Housing Policies for the Urban Poor

A Case for Local Diversity in Federal Programs

Raymond J. Struyk
Sue A. Marshall
Larry J. Ozanne

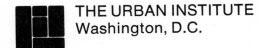

THE URBAN INSTITUTE
Washington, D.C.

FOREWORD

This study analyzes the long-term direct and indirect effects of several housing programs in a wide range of metropolitan markets. The analysis focuses on changes in the housing situation of low-income persons, but it also considers other groups and the condition of housing available during the year 1970.

The findings here are based on experience with The Urban Institute's housing market model from 1960 to 1970.[1] These findings contrast the actual 1970 situation with what might have happened had certain housing programs been in effect during the 1960s.

The main program considered is Section 8 Housing Assistance, part of the 1974 Housing and Community Development Act. Section 8 provides for direct cash payments to landlords for low-income tenants and gives localities flexibility in meeting their shelter needs. Also analyzed are (1) welfare reform and its effect on housing and (2) interest-rate subsidies for all new dwellings. The analysis then compares the effects—both actual and potential —of these three efforts with results from key programs for low-income people. Those programs are:

- Construction of more public housing;
- Interest-rate subsidies only for modest-quality (rather than all) new homes, which consumers can either buy or rent;
- Housing allowances, either alone or combined with a subsidy program for new construction or rehabilitation. (Housing allowances are direct cash payment to low-income households.)

Finally, the analysis projects the metropolitan housing situation in 1980, based on various trends and forecasts (outside the housing market model) that reflect the price of housing and the size and demography of U.S. cities. In addition, there are estimates here of how the 1980 situation would be changed if a sizable Section 8 program existed from 1970-80.

This study has three broad conclusions. First, conditions in

---

[1] The Institute model is an attempt to understand urban housing markets by describing how households, builders, government, and the existing housing supply are linked in various relationships.

individual metropolitan housing markets have a strong impact on the capacity of any program to improve the housing situation of the poor. A program can substantially increase low-income dwellings without raising the price of housing in one market, while having nearly the opposite effect in another, or a program can provide needed new construction in one market while aggravating abandonment in another.

Second, it is generally more effective to use a mix of actions to stimulate demand and supply than to rely exclusively on individual programs. The mix can include various kinds of cash payments and other actions that directly or indirectly increase the number of suitable dwellings for lower-income households. Today, only the Section 8 Housing Assistance Program includes both of these components in the same program.

One potential program in this mix is a major reform in the nation's welfare system—the kind of reform that would substantially affect low-income housing opportunities. Should the demand for housing increase because of such a reform, one could make a strong case for modest subsidies to suppliers to relieve any pressures on the housing market. Over a 10-year period, especially in the slower growing markets, this practice would increase the potential of welfare reform to improve low-income shelter without large increases in housing prices.

Third, the best program appears to be one that allows local variation in the mix of activities to stimulate demand and supply. The argument for local determination certainly has merit, given each area's familiarity with its own housing market and needs. Again, the Section 8 program, with its locally prepared housing assistance plans, could be a useful model if local planners have a sound understanding of how program mixes affect their markets. This book attempts to promote that understanding.

William Gorham, *President*
The Urban Institute

September, 1978

ACKNOWLEDGMENTS

Several persons associated with The Urban Institute Housing Group during 1976-77 made important contributions to this analysis. Mort Isler, the group's program director, made particularly useful comments on the Section 8 housing program. Belle Sawhill, Marc Bendick, Timmy Napolitano, Dave Carlson, Jim Follain, and Jean Vanski greatly improved various chapters, while Neil S. Mayer, Richard Muth, and John C. Weicher read the entire manuscript and made exceptionally useful comments.

Sarah James and Joan DeWitt provided background information on both Section 8 and the public housing programs, Steve Malpezzi assisted in the research and Joe Gueron with computer programming needs. Marilyn Whipple supervised preparation of the original manuscript. D. W. Gottlieb and Associates assisted with final editorial preparation.

The work was conducted at The Urban Institute and funded through the Office of the Assistant Secretary for Policy Development and Research, U.S. Department of Housing and Urban Development (HUD). However, the conclusions and policy recommendations in this volume reflect only the views of the authors, and responsibility for any errors rests solely with them.

CONTENTS

LIST OF TABLES

xi

LIST OF FIGURES

1
HOUSING PROGRAMS IN HOUSING MARKETS

This book is about federal housing programs, the cities, and the urban poor. How effective are current and proposed programs? What is the relationship between these programs and the rest of the housing market? These questions are posed for ten programs through the application of a housing market model, which portrays the links between these key market factors: households, builders, government, landlords, and the housing stock.

Current housing programs help only a few of the urban poor today. We ask how those programs would work if they were expanded. When programs are considered here, they are assumed to aid at least a tenth of the population of each urban area.

In this analysis, we do not deal with immediate, short-run program effects but consider only decade-long impacts, so that both consumers and housing stock have time to react to the programs under scrutiny. The 1960s are the backdrop for most programs because basic trends for that period are well understood. Some projections for the 1970s show how trends are changing.

What programs are analyzed? Greatest attention goes to the Section 8 Housing Assistance Program. Part of the 1974 Housing and Community Development Act, this program involves direct cash payment to landlords in an effort to help low-income families pay their rents. Also analyzed are an interest-rate subsidy for all new dwellings (regardless of their cost or the

1

occupants' income) and the effects on housing of major welfare
system reform.

The consequences of several other programs are then contrasted with those three; the others include construction of more
public housing, interest-rate subsidies aimed only at modest-
quality new dwellings for ownership or rental, and housing
allowances—either alone or combined with a subsidy program
for new construction or rehabilitation. (Housing allowances are
direct cash payments to low-income households.)

Finally, this study includes urban housing projections for
1980 and three major conclusions on housing policies and
programs.

The theme of this volume is that a national housing policy
that applies the same housing program in all urban markets is
a mistake because of vast differences in the direct and indirect
effects produced by any major government program. The remainder of this book documents the need for greater program
flexibility, based on the diversity of metropolitan housing markets
in the United States.

DIVERSE RESULTS OF HOUSING POLICY

What are the results of recent national housing programs
for low-income people? In the last decade, this question has been
hotly debated. In part, this debate seems to stem from different
views on how to achieve common objectives. However, some of
the debate stems from a lack of understanding of the consequences of certain policies on housing markets. Congress and the
executive branch, researchers and scholars who advise government officials, and representatives of various advocacy groups
all need an improved understanding of the long-run and indirect
effects of policies.

Consider a potential federal subsidy program to build
apartments for moderate-income households. Why support this
program? Immediate reasons are to help the building industry—
especially when it has a large excess capacity—and to provide
more housing for moderate-income households.

A more indirect and longer-run argument on behalf of
moderate-income housing construction is that it could indirectly
improve housing for the poor through the "filtering" process. In
other words, the poor could conceivably move into dwellings

)

vacated by moderate-income people seeking the better housing made available under the subsidy program.

Filtering could help cities with a chronic shortage of decent housing for the poor, a condition that often results from large population influxes. When there is an increase of more households at all income levels, it can be argued that the market alone will not supply enough low-income dwellings, especially where (in the absence of subsidies) local building codes raise the cost of residential construction beyond the reach of the poor. Filtering in the wake of new construction thus holds a very real prospect of relief for the poor in rapidly growing areas, although the process takes time.[1]

On the other hand, filtering itself can cause problems. For instance, if population growth does not accompany the new construction, filtering can lead to widespread abandonment of still usable structures in low-income neighborhoods and the eventual deterioration of entire urban areas.

This highly simplified example suggests several points that are important in understanding housing markets. First, government programs have notable indirect effects. Second, these indirect effects can vary sharply with conditions in individual metropolitan areas. In the example, such conditions included the size of the low-income population relative to the number of dwellings available to it, the projected growth in the numbers of poor households and other households, and the likelihood of dwellings being "filtered" to the poor.

Third, the size of a program is critical. Different markets can efficiently absorb only certain amounts of subsidized housing; introducing too much of it will produce such dislocations as the abandonment of still usable structures. Finally, the example also suggests that enormous differences in impacts of the same programs may be detected, depending on whether one considers only the first three or four years after a program starts or the longer-term perspective.

Reasonably good information is available on the direct, short-term effects of housing policies. The visible results are new units and the possible demolition of existing ones. But little is known about the long-term effects, both direct and indirect, of these policies in different kinds of metropolitan areas. Thus, the

---

[1] The filtering strategy is discussed by A. Downs in "Housing the Urban Poor: The Economics of Various Strategies," *American Economic Review* (September 1969), pp. 646-51.

real significance of shifting the balance between housing demand and supply is often hidden or uncertain.

Recent legislation has increased the need for this type of analysis. The Housing and Community Development Act of 1974 tried to shift to local jurisdictions the responsibility for deciding the best way to meet their housing needs. Under the Housing Assistance Payments Program of that act—the so-called "Section 8" program—[2] the local community can use federal funds to select its own mix of new construction, rehabilitation, and leasing of existing units. However, local groups, even with their intimate knowledge of conditions in their areas, are often unable to comprehend fully the long-term effects of alternative mixes. Clearly, analyses of the effects of housing policies could provide the guidance needed in allocation decisions.

Few such analyses have been completed because they are hard to conceptualize and implement. Yet, better understanding of housing policies and their results is possible. One approach is through social experiments. Thus, the Department of Housing and Urban Development (HUD) is sponsoring a large-scale prototype of a national housing allowance program in a dozen cities, principally to study the full effects of introducing this idea.[3]

This volume describes an alternative approach to analyzing the effects of a series of potential programs on the housing market. The analysis uses The Urban Institute's Housing Market Simulation Model of 10-year changes in housing quality and household locations in metropolitan areas.

Because of its simplicity and low cost when compared to social experiments, the model has recently been used to study a range of government housing policies. It focuses on the two areas for which the least information exists: the differences in policy effects among metropolitan areas and the differences between short-term direct effects and long-term direct and indirect effects. Furthermore, the model is designed to capture the impact of governmental or private actions on the housing situation of a wide range of people, who are differentiated by race, income, or family type (e.g., nonelderly families compared to single individuals).

Although the main analysis here relies on a simulation model, this volume does not merely describe an analytical tool.

---

[2] Title II, Section 8; 43 U.S.C. 1437f.

[3] For an overview of these experiments, see David Carlson and John D. Heinberg, *How Housing Allowances Work* (Washington, D.C.: The Urban Institute, 1977).

Rather, it is a broader analysis and evaluation of housing policies in urban America. Chapter 2 and appendix A describe the model, but other chapters consider a wide variety of current and potential housing programs.[4] Chapters 3 and 4 examine how various government actions would affect (a) the quality of housing for the poor and (b) other types of households and the general housing stock as well. The following three programs are considered in those two chapters:

1. Section 8's consumer subsidies, paid by local housing authorities under contracts of varying length to owners of new or existing dwellings;
2. Capital subsidies for all new residential construction; and
3. A general system of direct cash payments to certain households (without earmarking the money for housing), which could result from a major reform of the current welfare system.

In chapter 5, the model is used to project the 1980 housing situation in selected metropolitan areas. These projections are of particular interest in view of the sharp increase in housing costs compared to incomes in the first half of the 1970s. The final chapter summarizes the effects of 10 housing programs, including those analyzed in the earlier chapters, and tries to point out which programs would be best in different types of metropolitan areas. Some readers may wish to move directly to this discussion after chapter 2.

Before turning to the housing policies themselves, however, it is essential to understand the diversity of U.S. housing markets and the way these markets operate. The next two sections discuss these key points.

VARIETY OF URBAN AMERICA

Impressions of the nation's urban diversity are substantiated by examining the many contrasts among the approximately 250 Standard Metropolitan Statistical Areas (SMSAs) and the factors that determine the quality of their housing. This section documents differences among areas, and the next examines how these differences relate to various housing policy trends.

---

[4] A full description of the model is provided in F. deLeeuw and R. Struyk, *The Web of Urban Housing: Analyzing Policy with a Market Simulation Model* (Washington, D.C.: The Urban Institute, 1975).

Table 1 shows 15 metropolitan housing indicators, compiled from a random sample of 40 SMSAs. The 40 areas (listed in the table notes) are divided into four population groups to emphasize variations, even among cities of roughly the same size.

Population density and the percentage of dwellings in one-unit structures are closely related and provide a rough measure of a city's spatial form. The black population is depicted in the table's spatial form category because continuing and pervasive residential segregation in American cities constrains housing choices for both whites and blacks and often increases travel time within a metropolitan area.[5] All of these factors show enormous variations within each size category. For example, population density in the second largest size grouping of cities ranges from 314 persons per square mile in Dallas to 2,654 in Newark; among the smallest SMSAs, Lowell has a black population of 1 percent while Augusta's is 28 percent.

As will be evident later, one way to differentiate housing demand in various SMSAs is to examine growth in the total number of households, especially the low- to moderate-income type. The second set of indicators in the table shows housing demand. (Variations in median family income levels and in the percentage of households below the poverty line suggest the actual degree of poverty.)[6]

The percentage changes in housing demand for families during the 1960s (see rows 8 and 9 in table 1) show an enormous range. Note that both San Jose and Milwaukee are in the second largest group of cities. San Jose grew overall by 66 percent, and low- to moderate-income households grew by 25 percent. Milwaukee, by contrast, grew overall by 5 percent, while the number of low- to moderate-income families declined by 17 percent. Such differences obviously imply quite different demands for lower-income housing in the two cities.

The final indicators refer to housing stock and the availability of housing relative to demand. The percentages of units built in

[5] On the extent and persistence of residential racial segregation in American cities, see A. Sorensen, K. E. Taeber, and L. J. Hollingsworth, Jr., *Indices of Racial Residential Segregation for 109 Cities in the United States, 1940 to 1970* (Madison, Wis.: The Institute for Research on Poverty, University of Wisconsin, 1974), and A. Schnare, *Residential Segregation by Race in U.S. Metropolitan Areas* (Washington, D.C., The Urban Institute, 1977).

[6] These factors are only suggestive of the degree of poverty because regional price differences are not considered in these income figures.

the 1960s and before 1950 (rows 12 and 13) give some idea of the stock's vintage. Note that the proportion of housing built in the decade before 1970 is in no case less than 10 percent of the 1970 figure, regardless of the growth rate in the number of households.

The demand for new housing stems from both income and population growth plus depreciation of the existing stock; nevertheless, substantial new construction in the face of little growth in the number of households signals a potential housing excess in some markets.

HUD's estimate of the rental vacancy rate and the "fair market rent" of a two-bedroom apartment are included under the housing supply heading, although both obviously result from the interaction of demand and supply. Again, the range of differences in these variables among cities of comparable size is striking.

What does this diversity of American cities imply for national housing policy? To answer this question, one must identify factors common to all housing markets and explain how they interrelate to produce key differences among those markets.

WORKINGS OF THE URBAN HOUSING MARKET

A few factors at work in all housing markets can explain many differences across markets. The few factors to be discussed here are:

- Durability and immobility of housing structures;
- Existence of submarkets with differing prices *per unit of housing services*;
- Extent of new construction and population changes, particularly among low-income people.

One characteristic that distinguishes housing from most other goods is its durability. This refers not only to the fact that a structure lasts a long time—probably 50 years or more—but that it is comparatively inflexible, meaning difficult and costly to modify, once it is built. An important consequence of this inflexibility is that, in the face of demand increases, the supply of existing housing is slow to change and any change that occurs over a short time is small in comparison to what already exists.

A second characteristic that distinguishes housing from

Table 1
INDICATORS OF METROPOLITAN HOUSING MARKET DIVERSITY[a]

Indicator Spatial form	Population Size Category[b]							
	2 million		1-2 million		500,000-1 million		50,000-500,000	
	Maximum value	Minimum value	Maximum value	Minimum value	Maximum value	Minimum value	Maximum value	Minimum value
1. Population (000)	11,571 New York	2,070 Baltimore	1,984 Houston	1,064 San Jose	916 Columbus, Ohio	529 Jacksonville	413 Fresno	65 Midland
2. Pop. density per sq. mi. (000)	5,419 New York	788 Pittsburgh	2,654 Newark	314 Dallas	691 Jacksonville	234 Sacramento	1,076 New Bedford	69 Fresno
3. % dwellings in 1-unit structure	73 Philadelphia	28 New York	74 Houston	47 Newark	81 Youngstown-Warren	62 Syracuse	86 Midland	46 New Bedford
4. % of black pop.	24 Baltimore	4 Boston	19 Houston	2 San Jose	23 Jacksonville	4 Syracuse	28 Augusta, Ga.	1 Lowell
Housing demand								
5. Median family income ($)	12,112 Detroit	9,729 Pittsburgh	12,453 San Jose	10,129 San Diego	11,965 Rochester, N.Y.	7,473 Columbus, Ohio	10,934 Lowell	8,199 Knoxville
6. % households in poverty	9.3 New York	6.1 Boston	9.8 Houston	4.6 Minneapolis-St. Paul	14.1 Jacksonville	5.2[c] Rochester, N.Y.	17.4 El Paso	6.1[c] Des Moines
7. % dwellings owner-occupied	72 Detroit	37 New York	70 Denver	53 Newark	75 Youngstown-Warren	59 Columbus, Ohio	74 Midland	54 New Bedford
8. % change in families, 1960-70	22.2 Los Angeles	−0.1 Pittsburgh	65.6 San Jose	4.7 Milwaukee	27.8 Sacramento	4.4 Toledo	40.7 Gainesville, Fla.	0.0 Midland
9. % change in low-to moderate-income families, 1960-70[d]	5.1 Los Angeles-Orange	−23.5 Detroit	24.7 San Jose	−17.0 Milwaukee	27.9 Jacksonville	−18.1 Youngstown-Warren	15.3 Gainesville, Fla.	−17.2 Des Moines
10. % change in pop. 65 & older	11 Boston	8 Baltimore	10 Newark	5 Houston	10 Rochester, N.Y.	7 Salt Lake	13 New Bedford	5 Midland

11. Mean pop. per household							
3.3[b] Baltimore	2.9[b] Los Angeles	3.3[b] San Jose	3.1 Denver	3.5 Salt Lake	3.1 Sacramento	3.7 El Paso	3.1 Roanoke
Housing stock							
12. % of structures built 1960-70							
25 San Francisco-Oakland	14 Boston	49 San Jose	17 Newark	36 Sacramento	19[b] Toledo	47[c] Gainesville, Fla.	10 New Bedford
13. % of structures built pre-1950							
72 Boston	45 Los Angeles-Orange	64 Newark	21 San Jose	62 Toledo	31 Sacramento	78 New Bedford	22 Midland
14. Rental vacancy rate (%)							
7.9 Detroit	2.2 New York	13.2 Seattle-Everett	2.9 Newark	11.5 Jacksonville	4.6 Salt Lake	15.5 Midland	3.2 New Bedford
15. "Fair market rate" of 2-bedroom apt., 1975 ($)[e]							
241 New York	178 Pittsburgh	231 San Jose	170 Houston	210 Rochester, N.Y.	160 Jacksonville	216 Lowell	127 Beaumont-Port Arthur

Sources: U.S. Bureau of the Census, *County and City Data Book, 1972* (Washington, D.C.: U.S. Government Printing Office, 1973); U.S. Census of Housing: 1970, *Metropolitan Housing Characteristics*, HC(2) Series, and U.S. Census of Housing: 1960, vol. II, *Metropolitan Housing* (Washington, GPO, 1973 and 1963). Also see *Federal Register* (Feb. 12, 1976), vol. 41, no. 30 (Washington, GPO, 1976).

[a] Data are for 1970 unless otherwise noted.

[b] The areas included in each group are: (1) largest, New York, Los Angeles, Chicago, Philadelphia, Detroit, San Francisco-Oakland, Boston, Pittsburgh, and Baltimore; (2) second largest, Houston, Newark, Dallas, Seattle-Everett, Milwaukee, San Diego, Denver, Indianapolis, San Jose, and Minneapolis-St. Paul; (3) third largest, Columbus, Ohio, Rochester, N.Y., Sacramento, Toledo, Syracuse, Salt Lake City, Youngstown-Warren, and Jacksonville, Fla.; (4) smallest, Fresno, Knoxville, El Paso, Beaumont-Port Arthur, Des Moines, Augusta, Lowell, Roanoke, Lubbock, New Bedford, Ogden, Gainesville, Fla., and Midland.

[c] This indicates more than one city with the maximum or minimum value.

[d] These families are defined as 1970 households with incomes of $10,000 or less, compared to 1960 households with incomes of $7,000 or less.

[e] The fair market rent is the market rent defined by HUD for units to be leased under the Section 8 housing program. Such rents are defined for various sizes of units, all of which must meet certain quality standards.

other consumer goods is its immobility and, hence, the association of certain neighborhood conditions with each dwelling. Among these characteristics are the residents' racial and socio-economic status, the general condition of dwellings, the presence of amenities such as parks, and the quality of public services, especially schools.

An individual property owner exercises little influence over the neighborhood environment. At the same time, though, households have definite preferences for the types of neighborhoods and dwellings they occupy—preferences strong enough that they are willing to pay premiums to get the "housing bundle" they want.

These two characteristics—durability and immobility—make a series of closely related yet distinct housing submarkets possible within a metropolitan housing market. On the durability side, an excess supply or shortage of dwellings of a particular quality can exist for some time—that is, until dwellings are modified to meet demands. On the immobility side, similar demand-supply imbalances occur in neighborhoods, which are often slow to change in response to those imbalances. These conditions allow dwellings to command a unique price per unit of housing "service," as described later. Dwellings with similar price and location premiums form a submarket.

The concept of the "price per unit of housing service" is fundamental. To begin, think of all the housing services a dwelling provides. First are exterior and interior space—yard, walls, floors, etc. Second are major mechanical systems—water, heat, sanitary facilities—which can be further described in terms of their adequacy and dependability. While the list could be expanded, it is evident that one can catalog the major services a dwelling provides.

It follows that two dwellings providing the same total quantity of services could have different amounts of space, adequacy of heating, and so forth. Thus, one can construct quantity indexes that combine all these service flows into a single number. Further, if a dwelling's rent (the product of quantity and price) is divided by this figure, the result is a *price per unit of housing services*.

The submarkets mentioned before really referred to a case where the price per unit of housing services varied systematically because of demand-supply imbalances for dwellings of a specific type or location. Splitting housing markets into segments provides answers to many questions about how those markets respond to changing conditions.

An example may help clarify the origins of price differences stemming from the durability or inflexibility of housing. Imagine a market with only two kinds of housing: modest homes providing 100 units of service a month (as measured by the index just described), and luxury houses providing 200 units of service a month. Furthermore, suppose that the initial distribution of family incomes is such that the proportion of families choosing luxury houses over modest houses keeps the prices *per unit of service* equal in these two types of dwellings.

Then suppose that with the passage of time, incomes in the community grow and cause an increase in the demand for luxury houses. In the short run, the market would respond to this shift by increasing the price of a luxury house, compared with that of a modest house. Eventually, construction of new luxury houses and withdrawal of modest houses from the market when they are no longer profitable could restore price equality. However, in the interim, those families choosing modest houses would be getting a bargain in the price paid per unit of housing services. Because of housing's "durability," dwellings of modest quality could not be upgraded at a cost competitive with new units, nor would they be rapidly depreciated and withdrawn from service. Thus, an excess of modest units would result, driving their price per unit of service down.

Rising incomes, then, can lead to price benefits for lower-income households. However, it is easy to imagine other changes that would leave consumers of modest houses less well off. For example, migration of a sizable number of low-income families into a housing market might raise the demand for housing of modest quality, causing it to sell at a premium. Again, forces are at work that tend to restore price equivalency per unit of services in different kinds of houses: At high enough prices, luxury dwellings will be transferred from higher- to lower-income households or new, modest-quality dwellings will be built.

On the other hand, the forces moving prices away from equivalency can be stronger than those moving prices toward it for extended periods of time. Furthermore, in most U.S. cities and suburbs, the quality of newly built dwellings is strictly regulated; thus, increasing the supply by building new units for the poor is effectively prohibited. The only remaining source of increased supply—depreciation of existing dwellings of higher quality—can be a very lengthy process.

These dynamic forces combine with both strong household preferences and temporarily limited supplies of certain dwellings and neighborhoods. All these factors continually act to create price differences among areas or among particular types of structures. Moreover, there is no reason to expect the pattern of price differences to be the same in every city.

One way to demonstrate the potential for price premiums and discounts is to examine the changes in four diverse metropolitan areas during the 1960s. Table 2 presents data on two slow-growing areas (Chicago and Pittsburgh) and two fast-growing areas (Austin and Washington, D.C.). In the slow-growing cities, substantially more new units were built than new households formed, and there were major declines in the number of poorest households. Because people moving into new dwellings vacated their former ones, the supply available to low-income households rose sharply relative to demand, and this probably held down housing prices.

The lower prices would have allowed lower-income households to occupy better units while vacating their own. This process would have continued until the worst-quality housing was permanently vacated or converted to other uses. Of course, the extent of reduction in the price per unit of services for lower-quality dwellings of this type would vary according to neighborhood conditions, including racial mix, employment access to jobs, and public service factors.

Table 2

INDICATORS OF DEMAND AND SUPPLY FOR UNITS IN SELECTED METROPOLITAN AREAS

Indicator	Slow-Growth Areas		Rapid-Growth Areas	
	Chicago	Pittsburgh	Austin	Washington, D.C.
Ratio: percentage of units built to percentage change in households, 1969-70	1.40	2.11	.83	.72
Percentage change in the number of households with incomes under $4,000, 1960-70	—19	—20	—9	—13

Source: U.S. Bureau of the Census, U.S. Census of Housing: 1960 and 1970; *Metropolitan Housing Characteristics* (Washington, D.C.: U.S. Government Printing Office, 1962 and 1972).

In Washington and Austin, conversely, new construction did not keep pace with household formation during the 1960s. As a result, vacancies were rare and existing structures were usually occupied. These circumstances combined with a fairly constant number of poor households because of high rates of migration into the areas. Together, these factors produced an excess demand and rising prices in submarkets serving low-income households.

Population growth and rising incomes are not the only changes that affect the housing market. Another is the price per unit of service in new dwellings. Much of the existing stock must be priced competitively with new housing, since many people have the option of buying or renting either new or older dwellings. Furthermore, if the price per unit of service of new dwellings declines, more people will select new units, leaving their former ones available for less affluent households.

On the other hand, an upward shift in the price per unit of services of new dwellings causes a sharply reduced filtering of dwellings to lower-income households, even in areas like Pittsburgh and Chicago, because the higher-income people are more likely to stay where they are. This situation can lead to market-wide increases in the price of housing and even absolute shortages for the poorest people who might, at the extreme, be forced to double up. Thus, these indirect market effects of higher new construction costs can affect the housing situation of many more households than just the purchasers of new homes.

Variation in the price per unit of housing services for older and new dwellings may also influence racial segregation in housing. Black households with low average incomes tend to be concentrated in the lowest-quality housing. If that housing is substantially cheaper than new shelters, black families will not be motivated to move. In contrast, a low price per unit of service for new units encourages residential mobility for blacks and the poor by adding to the supply of available units and thus increasing the cost to those who refuse to sell or rent to blacks.

The main point of this and the prior discussion, however, is the fact that the prices paid by low-income (often black) households are sensitive to demand and supply conditions in the overall market. Indeed, the submarkets—as defined by the quantity of services that dwellings provide, by neighborhood characteristics, or by combinations of the two—are all linked. They are linked on the demand side through the behavior of households in evaluating alternative housing-neighborhood price combinations. On the supply side, the submarkets are linked by the response of housing suppliers to shifts in demand, as reflected in prices.

The central point of the argument thus far is this: The magnitude and type of indirect effects caused by an external change depend upon market conditions. This is true whether the external change is from population growth, a change in the price of housing, or, as will be seen in the coming chapters, the introduction of a new government housing program.

2
THE HOUSING MARKET MODEL AND THE CITIES ANALYZED

The conceptual basis of The Urban Institute model was outlined in chapter 1. This chapter shows how the model quantifies the concepts described.

DESCRIPTION OF THE MODEL

The model analyzes 10-year changes in the location of households and the price and quantity of housing services within a given metropolitan area. The 10-year period reflects a strong conviction that the quality of a family's shelter results from trends in household income, the price of housing services compared to that of other goods, and growth in the number of households and their expenditures on housing. A period of one decade shifts the analyst's focus from a host of shorter-term phenomena such as the building cycle and temporary rent controls to the more important elements just described. The longer period also involves a much simpler model formulation.

It is important to note that the model is calibrated to individual metropolitan areas. Predictions are thus area specific, and one of the model's best uses is applying it to diverse areas. This characteristic sets the model sharply apart from others that

15

are national in scope, such as models predicting the number of new dwellings built in a year.

The model operates at a fairly high level of aggregation: An urban area is typically divided into four to six zones, with each one similar in terms of housing quality, the travel times of workers living there, and the socioeconomic mix of the households. In addition, households and dwellings are divided into three or four dozen "model households" and "model dwellings," which are structured to reflect the incomes of all households and the housing services of actual dwellings. Each model dwelling in effect represents a housing submarket.

The principal data inputs to the model are the number and incomes of households at the end of the period studied, the housing stock at the beginning of the period, and average operating prices (e.g., fuel oil) and capital inputs (e.g., mortgage funds) during the period. The model's main products are the prices and quantities of housing services prevailing at the end of the decade, the number of new units added to and removed from the stock over the period, and the location of households among zones.

Figure 1 shows inputs and outputs to the model. The inputs, on the left, consist of the cost to produce housing services, plus information on the following:

1. *Model households*—Characterized by race, income, and type of inhabitants (i.e., families or individuals). These are the housing consumers, whose objective is to select the dwelling they find most attractive in terms of price, neighborhood, and services. Housing demand is determined by price and by the normal income of the household. All model households are renters; homeowners are assumed to rent from themselves.

2. *Landlords and existing model dwellings*—Landlords control all dwellings in the stock at the start of the period; the stock is characterized by its location and the quantity of services initially provided. Landlords are out to maximize their profits, and they follow a schedule of price-quantity offers consistent with that objective.

3. *Builders of new dwellings*—New units are built on demand (i.e., at a constant price per unit of service, assuming an infinitely elastic 10-year supply). As part of the solution process shown in figure 1, each household

Figure 1

PREDETERMINED AND INTERNAL FACTORS IN
URBAN INSTITUTE MODEL

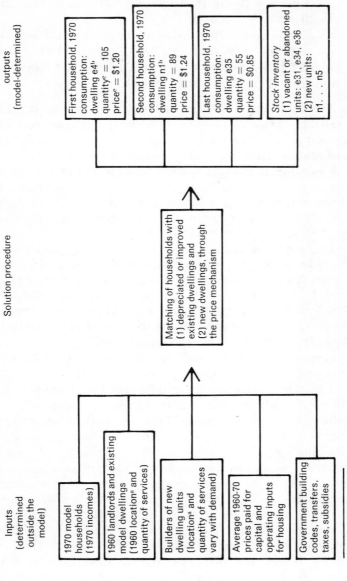

Inputs
(determined
outside the
model)

Solution procedure

outputs
(model-determined)

1970 model
households
(1970 incomes)

1960 landlords and existing
model dwellings
(1960 location[a] and
quantity of services)

Builders of new
dwelling units
(location[a] and
quantity of services
vary with demand)

Average 1960-70
prices paid for
capital and
operating inputs
for housing

Government building
codes, transfers,
taxes, subsidies

Matching of households with
(1) depreciated or improved
existing dwellings and
(2) new dwellings, through
the price mechanism

First household, 1970
consumption:
dwelling e4[b]
quantity[c] = 105
price[c] = $1.20

Second household, 1970
consumption:
dwelling n1[b]
quantity = 89
price = $1.24

Last household, 1970
consumption:
dwelling e35
quantity = 55
price = $0.85

Stock inventory
(1) vacant or abandoned
units: e31, e34, e36
(2) new units:
n1. . . n5

[a]Location is characterized by employment access (travel time) and race and economic status of households.
[b]The fourth existing dwelling is referred to as e4 and the first new dwelling as n1.
[c]Price is the price per unit of housing services; quantity is the monthly quantity of services.

considers living in a new dwelling that would meet its needs.

4. *Government*—The government can impose building codes and similar regulations, levy taxes, and offer help, such as price subsidies. Determinants of government behavior are not included in the model.

The solution process in the center of the figure consists of households choosing new or existing dwellings and landlords responding to overoccupancy or underoccupancy by changing prices and services. Households then make new choices, and so on. A solution is reached when no household chooses a dwelling different from the one it occupies, when each occupied dwelling unit has only one occupant, and when owners of vacant dwellings would receive rents too low to cover operating costs and therefore are not seeking occupants.

There are several kinds of outputs, then, as shown on the right side of the figure. For each model household, one knows the price per unit of service and the quantity of services consumed. By comparing services at the end of the period with those at the beginning, one can monitor progress in the improvement of housing. Progress can also be monitored for certain types of households (e.g., the old, the poor) and for certain locations (e.g., central cities). In addition, one knows the amount of both new construction and housing no longer used.

The model's framework emphasizes the characteristics cited earlier as distinguishing housing from most other goods: durability and neighborhood links. Durability enters the model through the detailed representation of the housing stock in terms of its quality and location at the beginning of the decade. Neighborhood enters the model through division of a housing market into zones where certain characteristics—e.g., travel times, racial and socioeconomic characteristics—are considered in terms of a household's residential choices.

Four assumptions underlie the basic structure of the model. First, households and landlords exhibit consistent, rational behavior. Thus, the behavior and relationships of groups or actors—like our model households and the landlords of the model dwellings—can be described. Second, homeowners act like landlords in deciding how much housing to provide and like tenants in deciding how much housing service to buy. Hence, there is no distinction between renters and owner-occupants in the model.

Third, the housing market is competitive, meaning that no

single landlord or homeowner can affect the market price of housing services, which are allocated among competing potential consumers by a price mechanism. Finally, it is possible for urban housing markets to be divided into submarkets for dwellings of different quality, in the sense described in the previous chapter. Different prices per unit of service may prevail among these submarkets in the short run.

Appendix A describes the model in more detail for those who are interested. The following section describes applications of the model to real and hypothetical urban housing markets.

CITIES ANALYZED

Applications of the Model

The Urban Institute Housing Market Simulation Model was applied to these eight metropolitan areas during the 1960s: Durham, Austin, Portland (Oregon), Pittsburgh, Chicago, Green Bay, South Bend, and Washington, D.C. These areas were chosen because of their diversity in several features thought to affect the way a housing market works. Among these features are SMSA size, structural composition of the stock (e.g., single-family units), rate of population growth, and racial and economic composition of the population. Summary data for each of the above areas (table 3) suggest the variety of conditions found there.

One purpose of the model applications was to estimate five of the model's nine parameters, the numbers that quantify the behavior of households and landlords. The estimated parameters are those for which independent econometric estimates have not been made before (including some for which such estimates are infeasible). Two of these are parameters of the landlord's supply function—the equation that shows how much landlords will change output in response to a change in demand.

Satisfactory estimates for these landlord supply parameters were not obtained through the applications.[1] Thus, two parameter

---

[1] Briefly, in the process of calibrating the model it is typical to obtain several alternative sets of supply function parameters that provide low error rates. These sets, though, can imply quite different degrees of responsiveness to demand changes on the part of suppliers. The ultimate choice among the competing parameter sets about which is "best" is often decided on the basis of small, and probably unimportant, differences in the error-rate criteria.

Table 3

SELECTED DATA FOR SMSAs USED IN URBAN INSTITUTE MODEL APPLICATIONS

	Durham, N.C.	Austin, Tex.	Portland, Oreg.	Pittsburgh, Pa.	Washington, D.C.	Chicago, Ill.	Green Bay, Wis.	South Bend, Ind.	All U.S. metropolitan areas
Number of occupied units (in thousands)	58	91	342	759	854[a]	2,182	44	76	43,859
Population density per square mile (in thousands)	274	296	276	788	1,217	1,876	302	308	360
Percentage change in population, 1960-70[b]	23	39	22	−0.2	38	12	26	3	[c]
Proportion of occupied units:									
Occupied by black households	.25	.10	.02	.07	.23	.15	0	.06	.11
Occupied by Chicano households	[c]	.11	[c]	[c]	.02	.04	[c]	[c]	[c]
In single-unit structures	.76	.71	.75	.72	.55	.47	.75	.83	.64
Occupied by owner	.54	.55	.65	.68	.46	.52	.73	.78	.59
Built 1960-70	.37	.44	.27	.14	.37	.20	.27	.16	.25

Sources: U.S. Bureau of the Census, *County and City Data Book, 1972* (Washington, D.C.: U.S. Government Printing Office, 1973); U.S. Census of Housing: 1970, *Metropolitan Housing Characteristics*, HC(2) Series, and U.S. Census of Housing: 1960, vol. II, *Metropolitan Housing* (Washington, D.C.: U.S. Government Printing Office, 1973 and 1963). *Federal Register* (February 12, 1976), vol. 41, no. 30 (Washington, D.C.: U.S. Government Printing Office, 1976).

[a]Figures are based on 1960 boundaries.
[b]Figures are corrected for annexations.
[c]Data are not available.

sets that bracket or include the range of feasible values are used whenever the model makes policy analyses or projections. These two sets are called *elastic* (responsive) and *inelastic* (unresponsive) parameter sets in the following exposition; the terms refer to the price elasticity of the supply of housing services available from the existing stock.[2]

Four Prototype Cities

The simulations reported in this volume were conducted for four prototype metropolitan areas; their design is based on the experience of calibrating the model to the eight actual SMSAs.

Hypothetical cities were used for several reasons. First, they could be so designed as to represent the entire population of U.S. metropolitan areas, whereas the eight actual areas do not. Second, it was possible to design the hypothetical cities so that the differences between them are few and precisely identifiable, making it possible to generalize about how these different conditions influence the effects of housing policies or key market trends.[3] Third, the four hypothetical cities could be designed to yield model solutions relatively easily and efficiently. Finally, because the hypothetical cities are based on national data, it is

---

[2] The price elasticity of supply is defined as the percentage change in housing services provided by a supplier in response to a 1 percent change in the price he is offered. The elasticity concept in the model refers to a 10-year period. The inelastic parameter set implies an elasticity of 0.5, and the elastic set implies a value of 1.2. These values include the relevant range found in the applications and are consistent with the small amount of econometric evidence available. It is perhaps worth emphasizing that these are the average values across all producers using the existing stock, and these values explicitly exclude housing services that are added through the construction of new units.

References to econometric analyses of the elasticity of housing services are: F. deLeeuw and N. Ekanem, "The Supply of Rental Housing," *American Economic Review* (December 1971), pp. 214-26; and L. Ozanne and R. Struyk, *Housing from the Existing Stock: Comparative Economic Analyses of Owner-Occupants and Landlords* (Washington, D.C.: The Urban Institute, 1976).

A complete listing of the parameter values used in the simulations done here are reported in deLeeuw and Struyk, *The Web of Urban Housing*, chapter 6. The values for the first six cities to which the model was applied are given in chapter 5 of the same reference; those for South Bend and Green Bay are in S. A. Marshall, "The Urban Institute Housing Model: Application to South Bend, Indiana," and J. Vanski, "The Urban Institute Housing Model: Application to Green Bay, Wisconsin" (Washington, D.C.: Urban Institute Working Papers 216-26 and 216-27, 1976).

[3] Every actual city, in contrast, differs from every other city in a multitude of complex ways; consequently, it is hard to know what might account for differences in policy results among actual cities.

possible to use various national projections by the U.S. Census Bureau and others in estimating future values of the model inputs.

The four protoype areas, designed to be representative as of 1970, vary in racial composition and in the growth rate of low- and moderate-income households. These two dimensions— identified while analysts were applying the model to actual areas as factors that strongly affect simulation solutions—significantly influence housing policy outcomes.

Racial composition is chosen because segregation is both a market characteristic interesting in itself and because it may prevent an efficient match of households and dwellings. The growth rate of low- and moderate-income households is important because it relates to the emergence of excess low-quality housing and, hence, to greater differences in the price per unit of service for that kind of housing than for other dwellings.

Because of the importance of these two dimensions, design of the four prototype cities began from a joint distribution of SMSAs by (1) minority group population rates and (2) growth rates of low- to moderate-income households.[4] This joint distribution was constructed from a random sample of cities in 1970, weighted by population. In fact, this is the same sample used in chapter 1 to illustrate diversity.

Four quadrants were formed by dividing the joint distribution of SMSAs at the median value for each of the two dimensions. The median proportion of minority households in 1970 was about 12 percent and the median growth of low- to moderate-income households during the 1960s was approximately 4 percent. Thus, the high-minority, rapid-growth quadrant is made up of urban areas with more than 12 percent minority households and more than a 4 percent growth of low- to moderate-income households. The high-minority, slow-growth quadrant reflects more than 12 percent minority and less than 4 percent growth. The low-minority, rapid-growth and low-minority, slow-growth quadrants are defined analogously.

One prototype city was chosen to represent each quadrant. The high-minority, high-growth city has a 20 percent minority proportion and a 12 percent growth of low- to moderate-income households. At the opposite extreme, the low-minority, slow-

---

[4] Low- to moderate-income is defined as $7,000 in 1960 and $10,000 in 1970. The two figures represent roughly equivalent purchasing power.

growth city has a 6 percent minority proportion and a 3 percent decline in low- to moderate-income households. Other characteristics of all four cities are given in table 4.

Each of the four prototype cities has a name that represents some distinctive aspect of many of the urban areas in its quadrant. However, by no means do all such cities in a quadrant fit the stereotype. For example, the high-minority, slow-growth prototype is labeled "Steel City"; it reflects the large northern cities with a heavy industry base which are common in this quadrant (e.g., Detroit, Chicago, and Philadelphia). Contrary to the name, though, Pittsburgh is excluded because its minority proportion is only 7 percent.

The high-minority, rapid-growth area is designated "Textile City" because of the many Southern textile cities in this category. Washington, D.C., and Houston are also included there. The low minority, rapid-growth prototype is called "Far West City" because many such cities are in the West and Southwest— for example, San Diego. However, others, such as Waterbury, Connecticut, are also included. Finally, the low-minority, slow-

Table 4
CHARACTERISTICS OF FOUR PROTOTYPE METROPOLITAN AREAS

	"Textile City" High-minority, rapid-growth	"Steel City" High-minority, slow-growth	"Far West City" Low-minority, rapid-growth	"Grain City" Low-minority, slow-growth
Minority households as percentage of total, 1970	20	21	5	6
1960-70 growth of low- to moderate-income households	12	−3	22	−3
1960-70 growth of all households	25	7	39	13
Number of model households, 1960	31	31	31	31
Number of model households, 1970	40	33	43	35
Percentage of all SMSAs represented by city	30	38	21	10
Percentage of total SMSA population represented by city	20	26	25	28

growth prototype is named "Grain City" because of the many smaller midwestern cities in this category.[5]

The next step in designing the four hypothetical cities was to compose populations of model households with the appropriate proportion of minorities and growth of low- to moderate-income households. The model households for all four cities were based on 1970 census data on the distribution of incomes in all U.S. metropolitan areas. These data yielded separate income distributions for the four household types distinguished in the model: (1) white nonelderly families, (2) white elderly households and single individuals, (3) nonwhite nonelderly families, and (4) nonwhite elderly households and single individuals. These groups were then weighted differently to construct the household populations of each prototype city.[6]

In all respects other than household characteristics, the four cities are identical. For example, they had identical stocks of model housing in 1960, based on the stock of all U.S. metropolitan areas that year. Specifically, each of the four cities had 31 model dwellings in 1960.

Table 4 shows the number of households for each city in 1970. It would be possible, of course, to vary the 1960 housing stock among cities just as the number and types of households have been varied. But because market outcomes depend essentially on household demands *relative* to 1960 stock, varying households alone accomplishes much the same purpose as varying both.

Housing in each city is divided into five zones, similar to those defined in the model applications. The first four zones contain all housing present at the beginning of the period. Zone 1 shows relatively low housing quality and a high proportion

---

[5] Appendix B classifies all SMSAs in the United States into the four quadrants.

[6] Specifying the number of actual households per model household for each of the four household types created a relatively small number (30-45) of model households with income distributions resembling those of actual households. The number of actual households per model household was varied within household types in order to obtain cities with the desired combination of growth rate and minority proportion.

For the cities with a high proportion of minorities, a smaller number of actual households per model household was used for the two nonwhite household types than for the two white household types; for the cities with lower minority populations, the reverse was done. For cities with a high growth rate, a smaller ratio of actual-to-model households was used for all household types than was used for cities with a low growth rate. Since the number of existing dwellings is the same for all four cities, there is more pressure to use existing housing fully and to build new dwellings in the cities with the higher growth rate.

of minorities in 1960; it represents the inner city of a typical metropolitan area. Zone 2 is an area of higher quality within the central city. Zones 3 and 4 are suburban zones, with the latter having a large share of high-quality stock.[7] Fifth is the zone of new construction, the location of all the new dwellings built during the 10-year span covered by the model. This zone's accessibility corresponds to that of a suburban location.

The four cities are also identical in the travel times associated with each and in the price of new construction. Our estimates of travel times are based on information for the SMSAs to which the model has been calibrated. In the hypothetical cities, it takes approximately 25 percent more time to travel to work from the suburban zones than it does from the central city zones.

Based on adjusted data from HUD, the average price of new construction per unit of housing services during 1960-70 was put at $1.24, or 24 percent higher than the average price per unit of service of the housing stock in 1960 alone. This $1.24 new construction price has two components: operating costs, set at 50 cents, and capital costs, set at 74 cents. Finally, the minimum quantity of services in a new dwelling, as required by building codes and zoning restrictions, has been set to correspond with the smallest new dwelling actually built in the 1960s in metropolitan areas.[8]

Most of the analyses reported in the following chapters are done for the 1960-70 decade, but some are for the 1970s. The values obtained in the 1960s simulations were used for the 1970 distribution of quantity-of-housing services. Hence, the number of 1970 dwellings in each area equals the number of 1970 model households (table 4).

There are six zones in the 1970-80 simulations. Housing built during the 1960s is located in the third suburban area (zone 5), and new construction takes place in a fourth, zone 6. Travel times and the minimum requirements for new units are unchanged, but household income and other factors are modified, based on projections to 1980. Contrasts between the cities in 1970 and 1980 are discussed in chapter 5.

Aging our original prototype areas over the 1970-80 period allows two types of analyses that are not possible from construct-

---

[7] The numbers of model dwellings in zones 1 through 4 are 7, 6, 9, and 9, with average levels of initial housing services (expressed in dollars per month at average 1960 housing prices) of 89, 94, 99, and 106, respectively.

[8] This was a quantity of services of 65 units per month. For an explanation, see deLeeuw and Struyk, *The Web of Housing*, chapter 4.

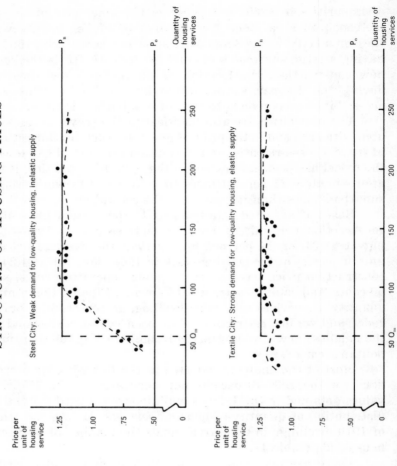

Figure 2

STRUCTURE OF HOUSING PRICES

Steel City: Weak demand for low-quality housing, inelastic supply

Textile City: Strong demand for low-quality housing, elastic supply

ing the cities as of 1970. First, the effects of a policy introduced in 1960 can be followed over a 20-year period, instead of the single decade simulated in a single run of the model. Second, progress or decline in the housing situation of groups of households that experience shifts in actual market conditions can be traced over the 20-year (1960-80) period.[9]

Key 1970 Outcomes

This section will familiarize the reader with the four prototype cities and show some of the properties of actual housing markets that model solutions capture. Price-structure curves are introduced in figure 2; these curves refer to "no-policy" outcomes —solutions in which no additional government actions are introduced beyond those actually in effect during the calibration period. The curves in the figure are actually for two of the eight cases (four cities and two sets of supply parameters) used in the policy analyses of following chapters. The upper curve in the figure is for Steel City, the high-minority, slow-growing area under the inelastic supply assumption. The lower curve is for Textile City, the high-minority, fast-growing area under the elastic supply assumption.

The horizontal axis in the figure shows the quantity of housing services per month produced by each dwelling, and the vertical axis shows price per unit of housing service for each dwelling. The points on the two curves represent specific model dwellings; they show how many services are produced per month and the price per unit of service paid by the occupant.[10] Each point of the curve can be thought of as the intersection of a

---

[9] There is, however, a penalty in this procedure in that the four prototype cities will become more similar over time. Because some fast-growing areas in the 1960s may be growing more slowly in the 1970s, the 1980 results obtained using this procedure will not apply to the faster-growing cities of the 1970s, but rather to those of the 1960s. Hence, the clarity of the prototype city is reduced by aging each of the cities to 1980. However, defining a new set of prototype cities has the disadvantage of reducing the comparability of 1960-70 and 1970-80 results.

Confronted with the need to choose a single approach, we followed to 1980 the original cohort of cities represented by each of the prototypes. The gain from being able to monitor the progress rate of groups of households (defined by income, race, and age) in a fixed set of cities was thought to outweigh the gains possible from more accurate documentation of the differences among types of cities for the second decade.

[10] The total monthly cost (rent including utilities) to the occupant of each one of these points is the quantity multiplied by the price per unit of service.

negatively sloped demand and a positively sloped supply curve for that range of services.

For most buildings, the price per unit of service (PPUS) falls somewhere between the PPUS for new dwellings (P_n) and the PPUS just sufficient to cover operating costs (P_o). P_o forms a lower bound on PPUS because a landlord makes more money by not renting a dwelling when PPUS is below P_o. P_n serves as an upper limit on PPUS for most dwellings because a household is very unlikely to pay more for an existing dwelling than for a new dwelling with the same level of services.

The important exception to this ceiling role of P_n involves dwellings with few services. New units cannot compete with these older dwellings because of building codes and zoning requirements. Below the minimum permitted level of new housing services, represented by Q_m in the figure, there is no reason why the PPUS cannot exceed P_n.

Dynamic forces within most housing markets tend to keep prices close to the new construction ceiling for moderate- and high-service dwellings. These dynamic forces are growth in real income and in population and depreciation of dwellings. All three of these tend to create excess demand for housing at the high-service end of the range. The result: The price of existing dwellings in this range tends to move toward the ceiling, and new construction tends to take place in this range of services.

In the low-service end of the range, the three forces do not act in the same direction. Growth in real incomes and depreciation of the housing stock probably tend to create an excess supply of dwellings in this range and hence lower their price. Population growth, on the other hand, tends to increase the demand for services in this range, especially when that growth takes the form of an influx of low-income households. Where the excess-supply forces dominate, the result can be a situation like that found for Steel City in the no-policy simulations. Where population growth is rapid and there is an effective minimum (Q_m) near the low-service end of the scale, the result can be a curve like that found for Textile City.

Table 5 presents no-policy outcomes for the four prototypes, considering both elastic and inelastic supply. Comparison of the various columns in the table substantiates the difference in average price associated with growth rates and with different elasticity assumptions. These differences in average price reflect differences at the low-quality end of the price structure curve, because the rest of that curve corresponds fairly closely to the

Table 5

NO-POLICY SIMULATION RESULTS FOR PROTOTYPE AREAS, 1960-70

| | High-Minority Areas | | | | Low-Minority Areas | | | |
| | Rapid-growth "Textile" | | Slow-growth "Steel" | | Rapid-growth "Far West" | | Slow-growth "Grain" | |
	Inelastic supply[a]	Elastic supply	Inelastic supply	Elastic supply	Inelastic supply	Elastic supply	Inelastic supply	Elastic supply
1. Average quantities, prices, incomes:								
Quantity of services per household	124.4	125.4	124.3	126.8	129.1	129.3	129.4	131.4
Price per unit of service ($)	1.186	1.230	1.129	1.190	1.194	1.246	1.160	1.216
Income per household ($ per month)	826.7	826.7	826.0	826.0	865.5	865.5	872.0	872.0
2. New dwellings and withdrawals								
New model dwellings	12	9	8	5	15	12	10	7
Withdrawals from existing housing stock	3	0	6	3	3	0	6	3
3. Location of minority households								
Number of black model households in								
a. Zone 1	6	5	4	4	1	2	2	1
b. Zones 2-5	2	3	3	3	1	0	0	1
c. Entire area (a + b)	8	8	7	7	2	2	2	2
Ratio, black to total households								
a. Zone 1	1.00	.71	.80	.67	.17	.29	.40	.17
b. Zones 2-5	.06	.09	.11	.11	.03	0	0	.03
c. Entire area	.20	.20	.21	.21	.05	.05	.06	.06
d. Segregation measure (a ÷ c)	5.0	3.6	3.8	3.2	3.4	5.8	6.7	2.8

[a]Differences in the elasticity of supply are differences in the way that producers using the stock of housing present at the start of the simulation period respond to changes in the price offered them by consumers. In the elastic case, this responsiveness is 1.4 times that of the inelastic case.

new construction price line in every case. Growth rates and elasticity assumptions also have a strong bearing on the number of initial-year or 1960 dwellings withdrawn from the occupied stock, with high growth and high elasticities both producing a relatively low withdrawal rate.

The prior discussion on price structure curves suggested that high growth rates should lead to high average prices and few withdrawals from the occupied stock. The association of higher producer responsiveness with these same characteristics does not follow directly from the earlier discussion, but it is not difficult to understand. "Adaptability" is one way to describe the housing stock under elastic, as contrasted to inelastic, supply conditions. Adaptable (i.e., elasticity-supplied) existing dwellings are capable of providing a wider range of housing services over the same range of price changes and can better furnish households with the levels of services they want. Thus, adaptable units are more likely to command high prices and less likely to prove so unsatisfactory that withdrawal from the stock is necessary.[11]

With respect to racial segregation, the fact that the cities with low minority populations have only two model households in the minority group makes it difficult to say very much about their racial residential patterns. In the two cities with high minority populations, there is pervasive segregation under both assumptions about supplier behavior. Black households are concentrated in Zone 1, the central city area with a relatively low quality of housing stock.

SUMMARY

Three findings in this chapter should be considered in evaluating later policy analyses in the book. The first concerns the structure of The Urban Institute's Housing Market Simulation Model, which incorporates the fundamental durability and immobility aspects of housing. As a result, the model explicitly allows for the existence of housing submarkets in response to supply-demand imbalances for (1) dwellings providing different quantities of services or (2) dwellings with particular sets of neighborhood attributes, especially the racial and socioeconomic characteristics of those living in the neighborhood.

---

[11] Adaptability also lies behind the higher average quantity of housing services purchased, in spite of higher prices, under elastic than under inelastic supply assumptions.

The second finding is that the model's portrayal of households as consumers of housing services and landlords as suppliers of housing services is based on extensive empirical evidence.

Finally, the prototype cities used in the policy analysis show a sharp diversity in two factors found to have important effects on the final housing situation of households: racial composition and the rate of growth in the number of households. Diversity has been limited to these factors to permit more precise explanations of the differences in policy results among cities.

3
ASSESSING THE LONG-TERM EFFECTS OF SECTION 8

The Housing and Community Development Act of 1974 created the Housing Assistance Payments Program, commonly referred to as Section 8. The program was designed to replace and improve upon a number of other housing programs serving low-income people. Although some characteristics of the former programs have been retained, there are significant changes in Section 8. The goals of decent, safe, and sanitary housing remain; however, direct funding to developers of low-income housing is not part of this program. Instead, the federal government helps low-income families pay their monthly rents through a direct cash payment to landlords. HUD hopes that this subsidy will be an incentive for developers, builders, and financial institutions to provide more decent housing.

Local jurisdictions now have more flexibility in meeting their housing needs. The program permits variation in the mix of activities to meet the needs of the low-income population. These activities can include building new units, rehabilitating substandard ones, and leasing acceptable existing units. The variations should depend in part on the housing conditions in a particular locality. Once the mix of new, rehabilitated, and existing housing is determined, the local agency enters into lease agreements with suppliers and uses federal funds to make the subsidy payments.

As noted in the opening chapter, the local flexibility embodied in Section 8 is truly innovative. For the first time, a community can effectively design a housing program best suited to its own needs.

Each eligible locality applying for a community development grant under this program must prepare a "housing assistance plan" that (1) surveys the condition of existing housing, (2) establishes present and future housing needs, and (3) indicates whether new construction is warranted by a shortage of standard existing housing. The purpose of these plans is to establish planning data and to relate the Section 8 program to actual local needs and housing market characteristics.

Housing units occupied by Section 8 participants must meet locally specified quality standards and must rent for no more than a HUD-established "fair market rent" (FMR). FMRs are designed to reflect local housing costs, as well as quality, location, and physical amenities. Separate FMRs for new and existing units have been established for each market (usually a county or SMSA); the higher costs for new units reflect the higher standards they must satisfy.

A national housing policy such as Section 8 can cause a wide range of market effects, both direct and indirect. In terms of direct effects, a certain number of new units may be built, the housing quality of participants improved, and their rent burden changed. Indirect effects, such as changes in the price and quality of housing for nonparticipants, depend in part on market conditions at the start of the program.

Efforts are now underway to evaluate how well the Section 8 program is working in meeting its legislative objectives. Most of these analyses focus, appropriately, on the initial experiences of agencies, developers, and participating households under the program.[1] The analysis presented in this chapter complements this work by addressing the long-run direct and indirect consequences of a sustained Section 8 program. Furthermore, while other evaluative efforts are analyzing actual program data, this work simulates what is likely to happen under the program. In sum, these long-term simulations are designed to help commu-

---

[1] See, for example, *Major Changes Are Needed in the New Leased Housing Program* (Washington, D.C.: U.S. General Accounting Office, 1977) and *Lower Income Housing Assistance Program (Section 8): Interim Findings of Evaluation Research* (Washington, D.C.: Office of Policy Development and Research, U.S. Department of Housing and Urban Development, 1978).

nities determine which program mix would work best in their areas, and to provide one part of an evaluation of overall program utility.

The first part of this chapter describes Section 8 and outlines how program elements have been translated into inputs for the simulation model. Also stated is the mix of existing and new leased units analyzed here. The rest of the chapter presents simulation results and summarizes overall findings.

SIMULATING SECTION 8

Defining the Program

Under Section 8, the federal government, by leasing new, substantially rehabilitated, or other existing housing, provides direct payment or subsidies for low-income families so they can afford "decent housing." The subsidy makes up the difference between an approved rent and 15 to 25 percent of an eligible family's income. This capsule description of Section 8 indicates three key concepts that must be translated into model inputs— eligibility, decent housing, and approved rent.

Eligibility is restricted to renters, and nonelderly (under age 62) single persons are categorically excluded. Families are eligible if their incomes fall below a certain percentage of their area's median income; this percentage varies with family size and is 80 percent of median for a family of four.

Limits have been set separately for families with "low" and "very low" incomes. Since the model does not distinguish among families by size, a weighted average of the income limits for "low-income" families of all sizes is used to determine the average allowable maximum percentage of the median. The weight used is the number of families of each size as of 1970. This average percentage of the median income—73 percent—is the eligibility criterion for all families in the simulations.

The percentage of the total population and the number of model households eligible in each of the four prototype cities, given this income cutoff, are shown in table 6. The number of households with incomes below 73 percent of the median is generally larger than the number that could be funded under the programs simulated, so not all income-eligible households are able to participate in the simulated programs.

The concept of decent housing is not tightly defined in the program regulations, in recognition of the fact that the same

Table 6
INCOME-ELIGIBLE HOUSEHOLDS AND THOSE ELIGIBLE TO PARTICIPATE UNDER ALTERNATIVE ALLOCATION SCHEMES

Prototypes	Total Number of Model Households	Income-Eligible Households[a]		Households Eligible to Participate[b]					
				Proportional allocation[c]			Fair-share allocation		
		Number of model households	Percentage of all model households	Number of model households	Percentage of income-eligible households	Percentage of all households	Number of model households	Percentage of income-eligible households	Percentage of all households
Textile City: High-minority, rapid-growth	40	11	28	4	36	10	8	73	20
Steel City: High-minortly, slow-growth	33	12	36	4	33	12	6	50	18
Far West City: Low-minority, rapid-growth	43	13	30	5	38	12	d	d	d
Grain City: Low-minority, slow-growth	35	10	29	4	40	11	d	d	d

[a]Income-eligible households are those earning less than 73 percent of the area's median income.

[b]Not all income-eligible households can participate in the Section 8 program because of funding limitations.

[c]Proportional allocation assumes that in every SMSA the number of households eligible for Section 8 is equal to 10 percent of the base stock of dwellings. Under fair-share allocation, a disproportionate share of Section 8 units goes to areas with a high percentage of minority households.

[d]No simulations were done under the fair-share allocation scheme for low-minority areas.

precise quality standards do not apply everywhere. For example, central heating systems are not essential in southern Texas. In reality, new units must meet a minimum quality standard under the building codes imposed by most jurisdictions. In the model, this standard is translated into a quantity of 65 units of housing service per month, based on census data. The minimum quality standard for existing housing under the program is set at a quantity of services that equals 70 percent of the standard for new Section 8 housing. This corresponds to the level of services provided by dwellings with the physical characteristics generally required to meet program standards.

In order to be certified as eligible for occupancy under Section 8, a dwelling must also rent for no more than the fair market rent. National FMR averages are used in this study for both new and existing units.[2] Recall that the prices of certain factor inputs for the prototype cities were based on national figures; hence, the price per unit of service of new units under the program is appropriately the national average.[3] FMRs for existing units are potentially somewhat more variable; however, an examination of those rates in the cities represented by each prototype revealed little variation. Thus, the national average was used.

The minimum quality standard represents the lower boundary for eligible units, and the FMR represents an upper boundary. An existing dwelling (one in the stock at the beginning of the period analyzed) must provide 45 units of housing service per month to meet the minimum program standard. At a normal 1970 price per unit of service, such a dwelling would rent for about $55 per month. The national average fair market rent for a two-bedroom apartment in an older dwelling is about $90, adjusted to 1970 prices. Thus, these rules define a rather narrow range of units eligible for subsidies under Section 8, a fact that has definite effects on program outcomes.

An eligible household can receive the difference between the

---

[2] FMRs for new and existing units were published in the *Federal Register* of March 1, 1976 and February 12, 1976 (Washington, D.C.: U.S. Government Printing Office).

[3] The national price per unit of service for new, unsubsidized units is used here. It is possible that the price of services in new Section 8 dwellings built under the auspices of state housing finance agencies may be somewhat lower because of the lower interest paid on the borrowings of those agencies. However, only 11 state agencies had engaged in such financing for any housing program by the time this work was begun. Thus, the market price per unit of service for new dwellings was used in this analysis.

FMR and 15 to 25 percent of its income, depending on its degree of poverty. In the simulations, all subsidies are determined using 25 percent of income, since it was not possible to make appropriate adjustments for family size. The program is financed within the model through a small income tax (less than 1 percent) imposed on each household. Certain exemptions are deductible, and these deductions are such that no eligible household is taxed.

Section 8 has other provisions that are more difficult to include precisely in the simulation model. One is that the neighborhood where leased units are located must meet certain standards. Another is the requirement that the program not foster concentration of the poor in certain areas. Because cities are divided into only a few zones in the model, these requirements are not included in the simulated programs.

A potentially more serious departure from the program is the way the model represents the mechanics of the subsidy payments. As noted before, the actual program involves a contract between a local housing authority (LHA) or other sponsor and a landlord. The household is able to choose a unit that qualifies for Section 8 in exchange for 25 percent of household income. The landlord collects rent from both the household and the LHA. There is also a shopping incentive, in the form of a cash payment, available to people who select dwellings with rents below the FMR ceilings.

The model represents this arrangement somewhat differently. The household behaves as if it were given a cash grant equal to the difference between the rent of eligible units and 25 percent of its income. This provides a direct shopping incentive to the household by allowing it to keep the subsidy payment not spent on housing. Differences in the results of this formulation will be small if the careful shopping provisions of the program work well, or if households generally occupy dwellings with rents near the FMR.

Possible differences also stem from the range of units among which eligible households may choose. The simulated program allows extensive choice among new and older units meeting program criteria. In practice, a smaller range of units may be under Section 8 contracts. Note, however, that having a lease does not guarantee that a landlord will have eligible renters sent to him. The LHA can have standby lease agreements on many more existing units than it will be able to fill with Section 8 households, and it pays only for the units occupied by program participants. (For new dwellings built under program auspices, the LHA does have some financial responsibility.) Thus, a substantial range of units should be available under the actual program.

Another point concerns the household's treatment of the subsidy. The Urban Institute model embodies the generally accepted view that housing decisions are based on long-term or normal income. This view holds that because many of the poor are only temporarily poor, they will value an income-based subsidy at less than its face value in making a housing choice. That is, the household knows that the subsidy will decline as its income rises, or that more of its own income (even if a constant proportion) will go to housing as income increases. Thus, the household will look for a unit that will still be suitable when and if the subsidy is reduced. This behavior, coupled with the shopping incentive, means that some households will not try to occupy the most expensive units under the program—that is, new units at the FMR ceiling.

In reality, some households have little or no expectation of increased incomes, and they might not behave in the way just described. However, recalling that each model household represents thousands of actual ones, some average "discounting" of the Section 8 subsidy into normal income has been carried out for all model households.[4]

A truly accurate representation of all Section 8 subsidy provisions would be most difficult to embody precisely in the model. However, the approach used captures the main features and closely approximates the program's intent.

Program Size and the Mix of New and Existing Units

The size of the program simulated is of great importance because it strongly influences the magnitude of indirect program effects, such as inflation. The model uses three to four dozen "model" households and "model" dwellings to represent an entire

---

[4] Actually, there is considerable evidence to support the point that many low-income households are only temporarily poor. F. Levy, in *How Big is the American Underclass?* (Washington, D.C.: Report to the U.S. Department of Labor, 1976), studied the income changes of those in poverty for a six-year period. He found that about 25 percent escaped poverty five out of six years and another 30 percent were out of poverty half of the time. The remaining group remained in poverty but incomes shifted a good deal. (Note that his sample excluded the aged and disabled.) Other evidence consistent with this finding is presented in T. Kelly, "Labor Supply and the Poverty Problem" (Washington, D.C.: Urban Institute Working Paper 958-3, 1972), and in B. R. Schiller, "Equality, Opportunity, and the 'Good Job'," *The Public Interest* (Spring 1976) vol. 43, pp. 111-120.

SMSA, so that each model household represents several thousand actual cases. If 400,000 Section 8 units, the total fiscal year 1976 allocation, were distributed evenly across metropolitan areas, at most one or two model households or dwellings would be affected in any one SMSA, thereby having very little effect on the entire market.

To ensure that the program simulated is large enough to have significant impact, the minimum number of model households and dwellings affected must be at least three or four. For dwellings, this means about 10 percent of the initial or base-year housing stock for the period studied. To achieve this, we have simulated a full, 10-year Section 8 program. Under this simulation, additional year-to-year allocations of 400,000 units are made to metropolitan areas, yielding a total of 4 million units nationally at the end of the first decade of operation.[5]

This 10-year program of 4 million units would affect roughly 10 percent of the total metropolitan housing stock (44 million units in 1970). The first scheme for allocating Section 8 units among cities assumes that in every SMSA, the number of households eligible for Section 8 is equal to 10 percent of the base stock of dwellings. This is referred to as the *proportional allocation* scheme, as noted earlier in table 6.

The second scheme is called *fair-share allocation* (also shown in table 6). Here, a disproportionate share of Section 8 units is allocated to areas with a high proportion of minority households.[6] This allocation is consistent with the fair-share criteria embodied in the legislation, because several of these criteria, such as low income and high rent-income ratios, are highly correlated with race.[7]

The allocation of FY 1976 funds to the HUD area offices was used as a rough guide in determining fair-share allocations. The guide is rough because allocations in any current year may

---

[5] This example ignores the legislative stipulation that at least 20 percent of Section 8 funds be allocated to rural areas; other Section 8 allocations go to urban areas outside SMSAs. To satisfy this requirement, the annual increment would need to be substantially larger than the 400,000 units noted in the text.

[6] The number of Section 8 units is based on the amount of Section 8 funds actually distributed to the cities from which the four prototypes were constructed.

[7] Section 8 funds are to be distributed partially on the basis of a fair-share percentage according to: total population, households with incomes less than 50 percent of the median, occupied units lacking plumbing facilities, occupied units with more than 1.01 persons per room, relative housing costs, and households with rent income ratios greater than .25.

not correspond closely to the actual 10-year outlays, and because funds can be spread throughout different types of SMSAs covered by the area office.

Allocations under the fair-share scheme seem to represent the most that would be given to cities with a high proportion of minorities. Using the same aggregate 10-year program of 4 million metropolitan units, 15 to 20 percent of the households in high-minority areas could be admitted to the program under the fair-share allocation, and proportionately fewer could be accepted in cities having a low proportion of minorities. Table 6 compares eligible households under the two allocation schemes for each of the prototype cities simulated.

In deciding which mixes of new, substantially rehabilitated, and existing units should be simulated, primary guidance might have come from the first-year housing assistance plans submitted to HUD by the time this work was being designed. However, these plans, which specified a nearly equal mix of the three housing types, represented intentions rather than actual execution.[8] Figures on the type of units actually included under the program on a national basis showed a nearly even split between new and existing units, with very few reservations for those rehabilitated.[9] These figures, combined with the small number of units rehabilitated under government programs in the past, led to the decision to simulate only mixes of new and existing units in this first set of Section 8 analyses.

In deciding which mixes to simulate, three factors were considered. First, as noted above, early program reservations were about equally split between new and existing units, suggesting emphasis on a 50/50 split for our simulations. Second, the model is not structured to permit useful analysis of small changes in this mix. Effecting a major change from the model's 50/50 allocation requires using new or existing units exclusively because there are usually only four model households eligible under the proportional allocation. Thus, the mixes simulated primarily

---

[8] The figures in those plans are the simple means of the fractions in each type of unit (i.e., new, rehabilitated, or existing) for a sample of 147 cities drawn by HUD. They are reported in *Community Development Block Grant Program: Second Annual Report* (Washington, D.C.: HUD, 1976 draft).

[9] Based on figures in the *Housing and Development Reporter*, (July 26, 1976) vol. 4, no. 4, only 5 percent of total Section 8 funds were reserved for rehabilitation. Revised legislation now requires allocations to conform with the housing assistance plans. Still, it seems likely that, based on prior experience, substantial rehabilitation will not play a major role.

include all new, half new-half existing, and all existing, though in some simulations participants were free to choose between new and existing units themselves.

A third consideration in deciding which Section 8 allocations to simulate was past experience in simulating new construction subsidy programs and housing allowances (cash payments directly to households). This experience suggests that some program variations should be avoided in certain markets. For example, exclusive reliance on new units in a slow-growing city would produce substantial abandonment and no greater improvement in low-income housing than other mixes would achieve (an example will be given in chapter 6).

These considerations led to the selection of a basic set of simulations for a Section 8 program where funds are distributed under the proportional allocation scheme, with a unit mix of 50 percent existing and 50 percent new. This is simulated across all four prototype cities under each of the two assumptions about supply responsiveness (elastic and inelastic).

This basic set is complemented by simulations in selected markets of all new and all existing programs, and one program in which households are free to choose new or existing Section 8 dwellings. Other simulations using the fair-share allocation repeat the 50/50 split and the all-new extreme, adding a variant in which rent ceilings are removed. Fair-share allocations are confined to the high-minority locales (Textile and Steel City), as explained earlier.

All simulations reported in this chapter are for the 1960s. Thus, the results of simulating a particular program variant give a view of how the 1970 urban housing situation would have differed if Section 8 had operated during the 1960s. Chapter 5 gives projections of urban housing conditions in 1980, and part of the work reported there represents possible changes produced by a major Section 8 program in the 1970s. However, more emphasis is placed on the 1960-70 results of simulating Section 8 because of the greater uncertainty which projections necessarily entail. These uncertainties are detailed in chapter 5.

PREVIEW OF FINDINGS

A preview of the major simulation results are given here to help the reader follow the detailed discussions in the next section, enabling the reader to skip that discussion if desired.

Perhaps the most important result is how the simulated program affected the housing condition of participating households. In general, participants increased their housing consumption significantly. The amount varied with market conditions and with the type of program and assumptions about supplier behavior, but, on average, participants increased their housing consumption by about 27 percent under the 50/50 new and existing Section 8 program simulation. Further, the increase in the quantity of housing services consumed is moderately sensitive to the mix in the allocation of Section 8 between new and existing units, as reviewed later.

Larger Section 8 programs, which increase the number of the lowest-income households participating, raised the average consumption increase about 25 to 30 percent beyond that of the basic program simulated. Also, removing the fair market rent restriction on expenditures increased both the participation of lowest-income households and the average housing services consumed by all participants.

Participation rates for income-eligible households were high, varying from 50 to 100 percent in the simulations. Participation rates were around 50 percent when eligible households were allowed to choose between new and existing units, based on a decision process that stressed utility and assuming a strong incentive to make long-term housing decisions.

New units under the program provide a greater quantity of services than most existing ones, but new units often would require families to increase their housing expenditures by more than they wish over the long term, as household incomes rise and subsidy payments are reduced. Thus, existing units were preferred. Competition for the limited number of older units meeting the program criteria was intense, and rising prices caused some eligibles to decline participation. Full participation is likely when eligibles are given greater incentives by the local housing authority to consider new units, and most of this analysis assumed the presence of such incentives.

In certain cases, participation rates were adversely affected by the initial price per unit of housing services paid by eligible households. For example, the price of housing services paid before Section 8 by eligible people with the lowest income was very low compared to the price for units meeting the program's quality standards. Such households often elected not to participate.

One criterion for program efficiency is the fraction of the

subsidy transformed into increased housing expenditures—
known as the earmarking ratio. In these terms, the Section 8
program was reasonably efficient, with 60 percent of all subsidy
payments reflected in higher housing expenditures. These ratios
were consistently higher for new units leased under the program
—often in excess of 1.0—than for existing units. Further, the
proportion of the expenditure increase that was caused by higher
prices for housing services, rather than by increased housing
consumption, was modest under nearly all the 50/50 new and
existing program-market combinations simulated. However, the
Section 8 existing program by itself did result in sizable price
increases in the slowly growing cities with elastic supply
conditions.

Other indirect effects of Section 8 programs were the
consequences for nonparticipating low-income households and
for the stock of privately owned housing. The structure of the
program largely insulates nonparticipants from deleterious
effects. On the one hand, the program is sharply targeted:
Dwellings must meet minimum quality standards, and rents
cannot exceed a maximum. The second condition places a lid on
the amount of price increase possible. This limited the number
of dwellings that could be modified profitably to serve eligible
households, and it simultaneously restricted the advantage (possible if rents could exceed FMRs) of participants in bidding for
units.

In addition, existing dwellings placed under Section 8 contracts often were few compared to the number of participating
households. All these forces together worked to limit the overall
market effects. Although price changes and the reallocation of
dwellings among households predominantly affected participants,
the mix of new and existing dwellings in the program alleviated
those effects that did spill over to nonparticipants.

The effect on the housing stock varied with the type of
program simulated. At one extreme, a program leasing only
existing units caused no increase in the number of units withdrawn from the active stock over the decade. On the other hand,
programs that used new housing produced additional market
withdrawals that equaled the number of new Section 8 units. In
part, this reflects the finding that the new units built under
Section 8 are not substitutes for other new housing. At any rate,
the cost of these withdrawals must be evaluated on a case-by-case
basis, and any judgment would depend largely on the quality of

the units dropped from the stock and the types of neighborhoods in which they were located.

Overall, being able to use both the demand stimulants (transfers to households) and supply-augmenting actions (leasing newly built units) is clearly a very important and valuable aspect of the program. It also can be valuable to shift the mix of leased new and existing dwellings under alternative market conditions.

We might also note here that the results of the limited number of simulations done for the 1970-80 period generally agreed with the main body of simulation results for 1960-70. One difference that did emerge was that participation rates were somewhat higher. These higher rates were caused by the lowest-income eligible households spending well over 25 percent of their incomes on housing in the absence of the program, because of rapid housing price increases over the decade. Thus, they were eligible for the program, although under certain market conditions in the 1960s, the same households would have spent less than the 25 percent of their income on housing required by Section 8.[10]

SIMULATION RESULTS

Three dimensions of the simulations—market conditions, program size, and program restrictions—are key determinants of the direct and indirect effects of a large-scale housing program such as Section 8. These dimensions are discussed in turn in the assessment of Section 8 simulation results. For each simulation, the direct effects of Section 8 are revealed by the participation rate of households selected for the program; by the average subsidy paid to participants; by the amount of that subsidy spent on or earmarked for housing; and by the extent to which participant housing improved. Indirect effects can be gauged by looking at the change in housing prices paid by recipients and others; the housing consumption of nonrecipients; and changes in the levels of new construction and withdrawals of dwellings from the market.[11]

---

[10] For details see chapter 5.

[11] A change in new construction is offset by an equal and opposite change in withdrawals in the model, since for any one city over one time period the number of households is the same under different policy simulations.

All Section 8 policy simulations presented here are stated in terms of change or difference between a "no-policy" simulation (one involving no new federal housing policy) and one including the policy under examination. Thus, the policy question addressed by this analysis is: How would the housing situation in a given market differ in 1970 from the actual situation if the policy had been in effect?[12]

Not all the simulations detailed in this previous section are discussed in what follows. Selected cases have been chosen to represent the full set of simulations. Appendix table D-1 describes all of the Section 8 simulations, and tables D-2 and D-3 report all the simulation results.

Finally, in discussing the simulations, it is convenient first to consider the decision to participate in the program by households selected as eligible to enroll. Then the three key dimensions —market conditions, program size, and program restrictions— are considered in turn.

Participation Rates Among Households Offered New or Existing Section 8 Subsidies

The top row of tables 7 to 9 and D-1 to D-3 (pages 47, 50, 59 and 134 to 139) reveal participation rates ranging from 50 to 100 percent. Less-than-full participation results in part from the way recipients value their subsidies and in part from the program structure. Together these results suggest, for reasons explained later, that many households offered a choice will participate in Section 8 existing rather than new housing. Others will participate in neither because:

1. There are not enough units available that meet the Section 8 quality requirements and also rent for less than the FMR;
2. They can find units failing the Section 8 quality requirements but renting for substantially less than the 25 percent of income that Section 8 requires them to spend; or
3. They prefer to buy better housing than they can rent under the FMR.

Simulations in which households are given free choice between new or existing Section 8 units illustrate the effect on participation of the way households value their subsidies.

---

[12] Results of the no-policy simulations are in chapter 2.

Columns 1 and 3 of table 7 report the results of free-choice simulations in two of the prototype areas, Textile City and Grain City. (Textile is the high-minority, fast-growing prototype, and Grain is the low-minority, slow-growing prototype. Here Textile has been assigned an elastic supply and Grain an inelastic supply). In both cities, half of those eligible chose existing housing and half chose not to participate at all. None chose new units.

One might think that all households would prefer new units since new units have better quality and their higher cost is covered by the subsidy. (Remember that under Section 8, a household pays 25 percent of its income for housing independently of the actual rent; the subsidy makes up the difference to cover the market rent.)

The reason many people reject new construction, at least in the model, stems from the conversion of any income subsidy (whether actually given to households or paid to landlords directly) into permanent income before the households evaluate their housing opportunities under the program. Given that housing choices are based on permanent or normal income and that households eligible for Section 8 fall in the lower end of the income distribution, any addition to current income (such as a housing subsidy) is discounted by most households in terms of converting it into permanent income.

In the two city examples at hand, households' permanent incomes would rise by less than the amount of the transfer or subsidy. Thus, participants would have to devote other income to housing in order to occupy a new unit under the program.[13]

---

[13] Because this is the key to understanding why new units are less preferred than might be expected, it is worth illustrating how the real cost of a new unit to an eligible household can be greater than the real cost of an existing unit. Consider a household with a *current* income of $100 per month. The household occupies an optimal dwelling before the transfer which rents for $25 per month and constitutes 15 percent of permanent income. The Section 8 subsidies for the minimum-size new unit and the minimum-size existing unit meeting program conditions are $50 and $25, respectively. The apparent costs to the household—i.e., 25 percent of its current income—are equal.

If the subsidies are then discounted by 25 percent, the subsidy values in terms of housing decisions are $40 for the new unit and $20 for the existing unit. To participate, the household would have to spend $10 more than the desired long-run expenditure for a new unit but only $5 for the existing one. In practice, the FMR for existing units is set above the minimum quantity so that very often the household will contribute no more of its own funds to occupy units in the existing stock under the program.

Table 7
SECTION 8 PROGRAMS IN TWO CONTRASTING MARKETS

	Proportional Allocation			
	Textile City:		Grain City:	
	High-minority, rapid-growth		Low-minority, slow-growth	
	Elastic		Inelastic	
Case Number	1	2	3	4
Program Type	C[a]	50/50[b]	C[a]	50/50[b]
1. Participation rate	.50	1.00	.50	1.00
2. Average subsidy	28.89	23.85	28.90	24.18
3. Earmarking ratio[c]—New	—	1.58	—	1.39
—Existing	.448	.474	.379	.376
4. Average percentage change in quantity of services				
a. Participants—New	—	26.90	—	25.52
—Existing	12.65	20.23	20.56	28.30
b. All households	.75	2.38	.30	2.57
5. Percentage of change in expenditure				
a. Participants—New	—	27.06	—	28.83
—Existing	17.36	19.30	48.74	47.26
b. All households	—.19	1.96	.94	2.43
6. Percentage of increase in expenditure attributed to price inflation				
a. Participants	25.11	.53	62.67	25.70
7. Average price per unit of service				
a. Participants				
1. Base or no-policy[d]	1.193	1.215	.837	1.127
2. Policy[a]—New	None[e]	1.24	None[e]	1.24
—Existing	1.245	1.187	1.092	1.013
b. All households				
1. Base or no-policy	1.230	1.230	1.160	1.160
2. Policy	1.239	1.211	1.178	1.160
8. Number of units withdrawn				
a. No-policy	0	0	6	6
b. Policy	0	2	6	8
9. Number of new units				
a. No-policy	9	9	10	10
b. Policy	9	11	10	12
10. Number of blacks in zone				
a. No-policy	5	5	2	2
b. Policy	3	5	2	2

[a]Households have free choice about participation in new or existing housing programs.
[b]Some households are assigned to new units built under the program.
[c]This is the ratio of the change in housing expenditure to the subsidy received.
[d]"No-policy" refers to the absence of new federal housing policies; "policy" means that such initiatives exist.
[e]"None" indicates that no new dwellings were chosen by program participants.

Recall that even the households with the subsidy are trying to occupy units consistent with their long-term expectations, in order to avoid spending too much of their own funds on housing or having to relocate when their income rises. In Textile and Grain Cities, existing dwellings are more in line with participants' long-term housing plans than the new Section 8 units are.

Why do some households choose not to participate rather than accept units under the existing Section 8 program? The explanation involves features of both the program and the market. The program focuses participant demand on a fairly narrow range of housing: Dwellings must meet program quality standards but rent *at or below* FMR. There may be too few dwellings that can satisfy these objectives if the program is sizable. Alternatively, some households may find bargains that fail one or the other requirement. The poorest households may find units that fail the program quality standards but rent for substantially less than 25 percent of their income. This occurs in one simulation in this chapter—case 3 of table 8—and more frequently in the housing allowance simulations of chapter 6.

Finally, households with incomes near the eligibility limits may prefer to occupy better housing than that affordable at the existing FMR, yet still not want the full expense of new Section 8 units. This is the reason for nonparticipation in cases 1 and 3 of table 7.

Simulations such as cases 1 and 3 give households a considerable choice and assume that people make their Section 8 housing decisions in a careful way, to achieve long-term satisfaction. As such, these simulations could be seen as representing an extreme situation. Cases 2 and 4, also in table 7, depict situations in which new units are selected for reasons that do not stress utility, as does The Urban Institute model.[14]

In these simulations, the same eligible households that would elect not to participate under many conditions are exogenously assigned (i.e., not by the model) to new units constructed under Section 8. In practice, this amounts to having households "steered" by the local housing authority to new units or recruited by project developers. Alternatively, households might not re-

---

[14] These cases do *not* correspond to those in which there is no discounting of transfer (subsidy) income. Results of such simulations would differ fairly sharply from those reported here in the incremental participant demand produced by the program.

spond to economic incentives, such as the one that encourages shopping, so strongly as expected.[15]

In the remaining simulations, eligible households have been assigned to new units whenever such units are included in the program. (These cases are designated "program type 50/50" in table 7.) Nevertheless, the results of simulations such as cases 1 and 3 suggest that many eligible households may be less anxious to occupy new dwellings than our remaining simulations show.

Program Effects Under Contrasting Market Conditions

The simulations used to illustrate participation decisions also provide examples of the central themes of this volume. These simulations show that the same program can have very different effects in contrasting markets, and that flexibility in program design can be used to alter adverse effects. However, the "50/50 new and existing" Section 8 program turns out to have surprisingly similar effects in the first two markets considered here, and is therefore examined further in simulations across all market conditions. As explained later, consistency of results under the 50/50 program is maintained.

Alternate Mixes in Two Markets. The two prototype cities used in table 7 are at the opposite extremes in their preprogram market conditions. Textile City has a very tight market with a rapidly growing population and a high-minority proportion. Additionally, in the case of table 7, its housing stock is assumed to be elastic, or responsive, to price changes. Grain City has a loose market because of its slow growth, a low-minority proportion, and in these examples, an inelastic or unresponsive stock.

Because of these differences, the no-policy simulations in Textile City find the price of housing services to be up near the new construction price throughout the market, while in Grain City prices are substantially below new construction levels for low- and moderate-quality dwellings.[16] These differences between

---

[15] "Steering" is not necessarily pejorative here. Section 8 regulations place the burden for shopping, arranging the lease, and doing an initial inspection of the unit squarely on the participant. Assistance from the authority may not only be welcomed but necessary for program participation by some. Further, developers are much more important than local authorities in tenant selection for new projects. Finally, initial evaluations of the Section 8 program suggest that the shopping incentive is not well understood by program participants.

[16] The no-policy results were presented in table 5 of chapter 2.

Table 8
RESULTS OF BASIC POLICY SIMULATIONS OF A SECTION 8 PROGRAM
(50 Percent New and 50 Percent Existing Units)

Allocation Scheme	Proportional Allocation					Fair-Share Allocation	
Market type	Textile City High-minority, rapid-growth	Steel City High-minority, slow-growth		Far West City Low-minority, rapid-growth	Grain City Low-minority, slow-growth	Steel City High-minority, slow-growth	
Elasticity assumption	Elastic	Elastic	Inelastic	Elastic	Elastic	Elastic	Inelastic
Program type	A[a]	A	A	A	A	A	A
Case number	1	2	3	4	5	6	7
1. Participation rate	1.00	1.00	.50	1.00	1.00	1.00	.83
2. Average subsidy	$24	$34	$33	$27	$28	$38	$34
3. Earmarking ratio[b]							
New	1.68	1.25	1.39	1.16	1.84	1.06	1.27
Existing	.47	.36	—	.44	.46	.65	.82
4. Average % change in quantity of housing services							
Participants—New	27	38	34	28	29	33	31
—Existing	20	20	—	30	25	42	25
5. Average % change in expenditure							
Participants—New	27	48	57	21	42	41	67
—Existing	19	19	—	22	25	51	64
All households	2	3	1	4	4	9	9

6. Percentage of increase in expenditure attributed to price inflation[c]							
Participants	1	9	29	0[d]	15	17	45
7. Average price per unit of service							
Participants							
a. Base	1.215[e]	1.143	1.064	1.231	1.139	1.092	.878
b. Policy—New	1.24	1.24	1.24	1.24	1.24	1.24	1.24
—Existing	1.187	1.115	None[f]	1.147	1.157	1.126	.970
8. Number units withdrawn							
a. Base	0	3	6	0	3	3	6
b. Policy	2	5	7	3	5	6	8
9. Change in the number of new units	2	2	1	3	2	3	2

[a]In program Type A, some eligible households are exogenously assigned to new units.
[b]Earmarking ratio is the extent to which a subsidy is converted into increased housing expenditure.
[c]This is the percentage change in price divided by percentage change in expenditure.
[d]The overall price to participants declined.
[e]This is the difference in base price caused by the participation of different households.
[f]"None" indicates no participants in Section 8 existing.

the cities cause some programs to produce substantially different market effects.

One such program is the free-choice simulation reported in columns 1 and 3 in table 7. Because no one chooses new Section 8 units in these simulations, they can be considered to reflect the Section 8 existing program. As such, this program injects an equal amount of housing demand into the housing markets of Textile City and Grain City. In both markets, 50 percent of the eligibles participate, subsidies average nearly $30, and roughly 40 percent of the subsidies are earmarked for increased housing consumption.

Market responses to the demand, however, are quite different. In Textile City, where prices are already near new construction costs, recipients face price increases of only 4 percent.[17] In Grain City, where moderate-quality housing sells at a discount without the program, prices rise by 30 percent, removing much of the discount. Housing improvements also differ between markets, but not so dramatically. In Textile City, recipients increase their housing consumption by 13 percent, in Grain City by 21 percent. Thus, the same program can lead to very different outcomes, depending on initial market conditions.

Next, consider the effect of supplementing the "Section 8 existing program" with an equal-sized program of "Section 8 new construction." The simulations of columns 2 and 4 in table 7 assign nonparticipants in the free-choice program to Section 8 new units. In each city, the average subsidy drops slightly because those assigned to new units have higher incomes. Also, the new units to which these households are assigned are about 25 percent larger than the existing units they would otherwise occupy, and their cost is sufficiently high that these households must contribute more of their own money, as well as their subsidies, to cover the new rents.

Perhaps the most important effect, however, is experienced by those participants in dwellings subsidized by the Section 8 existing program. In each city, this group substantially increases its housing consumption and faces smaller price increases than it does in the absence of Section 8 new construction. In Grain City, where prices rise 30 percent under just the Section 8 existing program, price increases are cut to 21 percent by

---

[17] Unless otherwise stated, percentage increases in price reported here and elsewhere in this volume are calculated from the average prices paid by recipients, as reported in the table entries marked "Average price per unit of service."

inclusion of Section 8 new construction. In Textile City, prices remain essentially constant instead of rising 4 percent.

The effect of adding new Section 8 units, then, is to increase the total supply of housing for lower-income people. As a result, participants in the Section 8 existing units can obtain larger dwellings and any price increases caused by the Section 8 existing program are moderated.

In Grain City, the increased supply is particularly useful in moderating price increases, and because existing housing prices are below those for new construction, no new dwellings would be forthcoming in the absence of Section 8 new construction. In Textile City, price increases are small even without the Section 8 new construction program, so the addition of new dwellings is less useful in thwarting inflation. Furthermore, prices for existing housing are already near new construction rates, so the private market is potentially able to supply new buildings itself if faced with much upward pressure on prices.

Because the number of households in a city at the end of the period analyzed remains the same under all program variations simulated, additional new construction must be offset by an equal increase in withdrawals from the existing stock. Landlords of the dwellings withdrawn are the losers in the increased competition for low-income households. Withdrawals reflect one cost stemming from the new construction: Units that would otherwise remain in use are withdrawn, replaced by new ones that— at least in markets with price discounts like Grain City's—rent for substantially more than the dwellings they replace. Thus the "price" of increased consumption in Textile and Grain Cities, and of price moderation in Grain City alone, is expensive new construction and more withdrawals of existing housing.

The effects of new construction can be examined further through simulations of Section 8 new construction programs without any additional units under the Section 8 existing program. Table D-3 in appendix D presents such simulations for the rapidly growing cities (cases D2 to D4 and D11 to D12). Basically, the effects of new construction in these simulations are the same as those from new construction in the 50/50 new and existing mixes for Textile City. For recipients, prices change little and housing quality improves, but withdrawals rise along with new construction.

In these rapidly growing cities where the housing market is tight, the increased quality required by Section 8 often means new construction and withdrawals by the private market. In our simulations, the private market can supply that new housing as needed, since prices are high in the rapid growth markets and Section 8 increases demand to an adequate level. Alternatively, a combination of the Section 8 new and existing programs in rapid-growth cities appears adequate to meet the demands for quality improvement with less abandonment of existing dwellings.

A Section 8 new construction program by itself has not been simulated for the slow-growth cities. In these markets, the existing stock is underutilized and priced low enough that complete reliance on new construction would be wasteful. Such reliance would also lead to further decay and withdrawals of existing units. However, as the 50/50 mix simulations showed, limited amounts of new construction in slower-growth markets can be useful in holding down prices and increasing recipients' housing quality.

The effects of other new construction programs will be discussed in more detail in chapters 4 and 6.

The simulations discussed so far have shown that one program—in this case, a Section 8 existing program—can have greatly different effects in contrasting markets. The simulations also show that another program—the 50/50 mix of new and existing units under Section 8—can moderate these effects in both markets. In fact, under the latter program, increases in housing consumption and prices are more similar than might be expected in different markets. The following section describes this phenomenon.

One Program in Four Markets. The similarity of outcomes for the 50/50 mix of new and existing Section 8 units holds under a variety of market conditions. For example, cases 1, 2, 4, and 5 of table 8 show the 50/50 program across all four cities, based on proportional allocation and the assumption of an elastic housing supply.[18] All four markets have 100 percent participation, primarily because half the households are assigned to units built under Section 8 auspices.

All markets also experience a strikingly similar increase in recipients' housing consumption—25 to 30 percent. The earmarking ratios are consistently high for new units; even for existing units, about half of the subsidy is being converted into housing expenditures. On this basis, the 50/50 program appears to be very efficient in all markets. Another similarity is the

---

[18] Case 1 for Textile City is the same as Case 2 in the preceding table 7.

generally small proportion of increased expenditures because of
price inflation (entry 6 in the table).

Why are these effects so similar in such diverse markets?
To understand what is happening, look at the changes in the
price of housing services for participants. When simulating the
effects of introducing other major programs, price changes have
consistently been the volatile factor across markets. In these
other simulations, participants in markets associated with discounted prices for lower-quality housing—based on slower
growth of low-income households and low price elasticities of
supply—are more prone to experience price increases. The reason
is that in such situations, suppliers improve their dwellings in
response to program pressure for better housing and this
improvement often results in price increases.

This process is stopped when the supply of units in the
low-quality range is increased through the process of filtering,
as occurs with the construction of new Section 8 units.[19] In
markets with discounted prices for low-quality housing, the new
construction feature of the program offsets the price effects of
increased demand and encourages increased consumption. In
cities where the price of low-quality housing is already high, the
price increase generally is not possible, but filtering can still
occur.

One City, Two Elasticities. Another comparison of market
conditions is that of elastic compared to inelastic supply—cases
2 and 3 of table 8, for example. One important difference is in
the participation rate, and that difference stems from the variation in initial prices faced by eligible households. The inelastic
case 3 has the lower average initial price level for lower-quality
units. None of the eligible households chooses to occupy Section 8
existing units because lower-quality housing sells cheaply, but a
very large increase in expenditure is required to meet program
standards.[20]

Program Effects on Nonparticipants. When Section 8 is available, what happens to the price of housing and the housing

---

[19] As discussed in chapter 1, filtering is the process by which the poor
move into dwellings vacated by moderate-income people who seek better
housing.

[20] See the previous discussion of participation. Also, tentative evidence
suggests that some tenants may face substantial rent increases in order to
participate in Section 8. An example from Newark suggests that a family
now paying $180 a month in a rundown building without a subsidy could
pay as much as $280 as its share of the rent under Section 8 regulations.
See *Housing and Development Reporter* (October 18, 1976), vol. 4, no. 10.

consumption of nonparticipants (both eligible and ineligible) who normally compete with Section 8 program participants for the same housing?

Although data to address this question are not included separately in the tables, the simulation results were quite clear: Nonparticipants are little affected by the program. For programs simulated under the proportional allocation system, the quantity of housing services of nonparticipants increases or remains constant. Moreover, price increases over what they would have been are below 5 percent under all market conditions and elasticity assumptions.

For the fair-share allocation scheme, the changes are somewhat larger on average in the high-minority areas, where almost twice as many households participate under fair-share as under proportional allocation. Still, the increases in price and decreases in consumption never exceed 7 percent.

The small size of the market effects on nonparticipants is largely attributable to the structure of the program, which is sharply targeted by quality standards and FMR ceilings. The latter factor places a direct lid on the extent of price increase for eligible units. In addition, indirect relief of price pressures is often provided by new Section 8 units, which augment the supply of eligible dwellings.

Summary of Market Influences on Policy Results. Overall, we conclude that market conditions influence policy outcomes. However, the influence under a Section 8 program that leases equivalent numbers of new and existing units is less decisive than the effects of only a Section 8 existing-unit program. The reason for the lesser effect is the fact that by operating to augment supply (through new units) while raising demand (through transfer payments), a 50/50 program alleviates most market pressures.

Effects of Program Size

Differences in market effects caused by increasing a program's size can be seen by examining several cases for Steel City, the slow-growing area with a large minority population. In particular, see table 8, cases 2 and 3 compared to cases 6 and 7. Cases 2 and 3 involve the proportional allocation scheme with four model households eligible, while cases 6 and 7 involve the fair-share allocation scheme and have 50 percent more model households eligible.

Increasing the size of the Section 8 program while controlling for market conditions and program variation does not generally cause sharply different effects. Using a housing allowance program for comparison, doubling the size of the allowance program has much more drastic effects on prices for participants than are observed in simulating Section 8.[21] In the present simulations, increasing the size of the program generally caused the percentage change in the price per unit of service for participants to increase modestly, and prices never increased more than 30 percent beyond their level in the absence of the program.

In some instances, such as in case 7, a substantial proportion of the subsidy for existing units went to price increase, but consumption still rose by 25 percent. The larger price changes are again associated with the initial discounting of the price of lower-quality housing, which cases 3 and 7 illustrate. (Both assume inelastic supply responsiveness and have relatively low base prices for participants.)

The larger program makes more of the lowest-income households eligible for existing housing under the program. Most of these households participate, leading to large increases in housing consumption. In several cases, consumption for participants in existing units rises by more than 40 percent (entry 4 in table 7).[22]

Increasing household eligibility may not, however, always result in an equal increase in participation. Less-than-full participation in the cases simulated under the assumption of inelastic supplier responsiveness can be attributed to the low prices that eligible households are paying for housing when the program is implemented. As noted earlier, an eligible household may not want to increase expenditures on housing to 25 percent of its income in order to participate in the Section 8 program.

On balance, these results show that a program allocating a larger number of Section 8 dwellings than under the proportional allocation plan would seem feasible in terms of the side effects it produces in the market. Under the 50 percent new/50 percent existing allocation, at least, the larger allocations would improve program effectiveness by increasing participation and housing consumption.

---

[21] See deLeeuw and Struyk, *The Web of Urban Housing*, chapter 6.
[22] Also see Cases C13 and C14 in table D-2, appendix D.

Effects of Program Restrictions: Removing the Fair Market Rent Ceiling on Rents

Since the initial formulation of the Section 8 program, it has been argued that prohibiting participants from spending more than the fair market rent for housing, while also holding the government subsidy constant, reduces program effectiveness. The main argument is that housing consumption is held below the level desired by some participants and hence some potential housing improvement is not achieved.[23] Some cases discussed earlier in this chapter might have shown reduced participation rates because of this feature. In this final part of the analysis of Section 8, we explore a major change in its current structure by analyzing the effects of removing the FMR ceiling on rents.

Case 1 in table 9 repeats the free-choice simulation, with the FMR ceiling from case 1 in table 7. The fair market rent ceiling is removed in case 2, but the maximum government contribution based on the FMR is maintained. This means that, unlike the actual program, households are allowed to participate if they occupy a unit with a rent greater than the FMR. In this simulation, households are allowed free choice between new and existing housing as well as nonparticipation; for this reason, the results are not strictly comparable with those of the 50/50 mix simulations under the fair-share allocation.

The simulation results show that the participation rate is slightly higher when the FMR ceiling is removed than in the free-choice model under proportional allocation (case 1). A larger proportion of the eligible households choose existing units over nonparticipation. None of the eligible households select new units. The participation effect of removing the ceiling is modest because the two eligible households in the model that exceed the FMR on existing units are spending more than 25 percent of their income on housing. Hence, they fail to qualify for the subsidy even when the FMR is removed, and they also elect not to occupy a new Section 8 unit. The increase in participation, then, is completely among the households with the lowest incomes.

Examining the housing expenditures of these households shows that participation would have been lower if the ceiling were in effect. Average subsidies, as expected, rise in the absence of the FMR ceiling, since two lower-income households are the

---

[23] J. E. Goedert and J. E. Goodman, Jr., "Reviewing the Rent Ceiling in the Section 8 (Existing Housing) Program: Evidence from the Experimental Housing Allowance Program" (Washington, D.C.: Urban Institute Working Paper 240-1, 1976).

Table 9
POLICY VARIATIONS: SELECTED RESULTS FOR SECTION 8 PROGRAMS
(Fair-Share Allocation) [a]

	Textile city: High-minority, Rapid-growth	
Program Type Case Number	FMR Ceiling[b] Free Choice[c] 1	No FMR Ceiling Free Choice[c] 2
1. Participation rate	.50	.75
2. Average subsidy	$29	$41
3. Earmarking ratio		
New	—	—
Existing	.45	.660
4. Average % change in quantity of housing services		
Participants—New	—	—
—Existing	13	32
5. Average % change in expenditures		
a. Participants—New	—	—
—Existing	17	43
b. All households	0	3
6. % of increase in expenditure attributed to price inflation		
Participants	25	21
7. Average price per unit of service[d]		
Participants		
Base	1.193	1.214
Policy—New	—	—
—Existing	1.245	1.325
8. Number of units withdrawn		
Base	0	0
Policy[d]	0	3
9. Change in the number of new units	0	3

[a]All simulations in this table are under elastic supply assumptions.
[b]Proportional allocation occurs.
[c]Eligible households have free choice of new or existing Section 8.
[d]Differences in base prices for participants arise from differences in participation rates.

marginal participants. The consumption of participants is also greater than under the proportional allocation simulations, where full choice is permitted and is of the same order of magnitude as under the 50/50, fair-share allocation.

4
EFFECTS OF WELFARE REFORM AND GENERAL CONSTRUCTION SUBSIDIES ON HOUSING THE POOR

Federal programs not specifically aimed at housing for low-income people nonetheless can have a significant impact on the shelter needs of those individuals. Many needy households, for example, receive assistance through programs such as Aid to Families With Dependent Children (AFDC), food stamps, and Medicaid. Some of this money can be used for housing, either directly (as in the AFDC program) or indirectly, as a result of freeing for housing income that would otherwise be spent on food and health care.

Federal efforts directed to other groups and sectors of the economy also can have an effect on the housing needs of low-income households. For instance, low interest rates and new highways that open up suburban land to development can reduce the costs of new housing. In the 1950s and 1960s, these two factors encouraged much new building in the suburbs for high- and middle-income people. Through filtering, the new construction made older homes available to lower-income families. In the 1970s, high interest rates, environmental controls, and land use planning have had the opposite effect, increasingly forcing the poor to compete with the more affluent for existing dwellings.

This chapter presents simulations of two possible federal programs that could affect significantly the housing conditions of the poor. The first is income maintenance, a welfare reform option that would increase poor households' demand for housing by adding to their total income. The second program is a reduction in the mortgage interest rate for all new housing construction. This reduction could come about through a general reduction in interest rates as inflation abates, or it could result from a government-inspired attempt to stimulate the construction industry, especially in response to the periodic high rate of unemployment in that industry. This program would increase the supply of shelter for poor households by adding to the total amount of housing available.

These programs are simulated in two of the prototype cities used to analyze the Section 8 housing program. In the simulation, both "Textile City" and "Steel City" have large minority populations, but the former experiences rapid growth during the 1960s, while Steel City grows slowly. The existing stock of dwellings in Textile City is assumed to be responsive to changes in demand—i.e., it is elastic, while the existing stock in Steel City is assumed to be inelastic.

The high growth rate in Textile City makes the housing market tight, and the fact that its stock responds to demand means that dwellings provide close to what each household wants at the price families are willing to pay. Together these factors imply that the existing stock in Textile City will be extensively used and that prices there will be high even if there are no new programs. Conversely, the slow growth and unresponsive stock in Steel City mean that existing dwellings will be used at less than capacity and, in the absence of additional housing programs, will be priced low compared to new housing.

The two program simulations are drawn up for the 1960s and compared with the Section 8 simulations for the same period. The characteristics assigned to both prototype cities include those existing in many U.S. metropolitan areas today, as well as during the 1960s.

PREVIEW OF FINDINGS

As in Chapter 3, a preview of the major simulation results are given here. The reader may either use them as a guide in the detailed discussion which follows or go directly from this section to Chapter 5.

In comparing all three programs discussed in this chapter, Section 8 provides the most housing improvement for low-income households per dollar of subsidy, and does so consistently across markets. The program does this through the housing consumption requirements it places on recipients and through the leasing of new dwellings. Income maintenance also leads to significant housing improvements, but it requires a much larger subsidy. The mortgage interest subsidy for new construction brings about the least improvement in housing quality, but it causes reductions in the price all households pay for their shelter.

The income maintenance program results in noticeable housing price increases for recipients when the existing housing supply cannot meet increased demands for housing improvements. The Section 8 program moderates housing price increases through increased new construction but also results in greater withdrawals of existing housing.

Low-income households would prefer the income maintenance program because it provides more money and imposes no restrictions. How the target population would feel about the mortgage interest subsidy, compared to assistance through Section 8, is unclear. From the interest reduction, they experience modest savings on their housing costs and can spend these savings as they please. Under Section 8, the subsidies are larger but they must be spent on increased housing.

Finally, two of the programs have drawbacks in terms of economic efficiency. By lowering the price of new housing to consumers below a unit's actual cost, the interest subsidy encourages the production of more new housing than is warranted, thereby drawing resources away from other types of shelter and leading to premature abandonment of existing dwellings. Similar waste occurs under Section 8 when new construction is favored over the use of adequate existing dwellings, as occurs in the simulations for the slow-growing Steel City. The income maintenance program avoids these losses because it does not subsidize or require new construction.

INCOME MAINTENANCE PROGRAM

An income maintenance program would provide larger subsidies than would direct housing assistance programs like

Section 8 but, in contrast to Section 8 restrictions, this plan would allow recipients to spend their subsidies as they liked. The major questions are how much of the income subsidies would be spent on housing and what effect these expenditures would have on the housing market.

The income maintenance program guarantees everyone at least a poverty-level income. The subsidy equals the poverty level for households with no earned income of their own, and falls by 60 cents for every dollar of earnings. Families with 1969 incomes above $6,240 and single persons or elderly couples with 1969 incomes above $3,300 receive no subsidy. In terms of 1976 dollars, the two income cutoffs are $9,735 and $5,115, respectively.

This income maintenance program is similar to many recent proposals for overhaul of the welfare system, including the Carter Administration's proposal, except that it has no work requirements and no provision for public sector employment. The Carter Administration proposal has income cutoffs of $8,800 for families and $4,800 for single persons or elderly couples. The Nixon Administration's family assistance plan and the McGovern campaign's "demogrant" proposal were similar.

The government also is experimenting with several negative income tax programs that use the same subsidy formula. In addition, the Brookings Institution's report on the 1975 federal budget includes a thorough discussion of a national income maintenance program and presents national cost estimates provived by The Urban Institute.[1] The poverty-line support level used in the simulations reported here is at the high end of the range of those proposed, but these simulations relate to SMSAs, which have higher housing costs than do nonmetropolitan areas.

Table 10 presents the results of our income maintenance simulations and compares them with results of the Section 8 programs simulated in the last chapter, using the proportional and fair-share fund allocation schemes. The income maintenance program is larger than either of the Section 8 programs. Subsidies average three to four times those in Section 8, and every household eligible for the program participates. (Some eligible households do not participate in Section 8 because of the smaller subsidies and the imposition of minimum quality standards and maximum rents.)

---

[1] B. Blechman, E. Gramlich, and R. Hartman, *Setting National Priorities: The 1975 Budget* (The Brookings Institution, Washington, D.C., 1974) pp. 199-205.

Table 10

COMPARISON OF RESULTS FROM INCOME MAINTENANCE AND SECTION 8 PROGRAM SIMULATIONS (1960s)

	"Textile City" (Rapid-growth, elastic housing supply)			"Steel City" (Slow-growth, inelastic housing supply)		
	Income mainte-nance	Small Section 8[a]	Large Section 8[a]	Income mainte-nance	Small Section 8[a]	Large Section 8[a]
Eligibles						
Households eligible (%)	26	10	20	24	12	18
Participation rate among eligibles	1.0	1.0	1.0	1.0	.50	.83
Recipients						
Average subsidy ($)	102	24	43	116	33	34
Earmarking ratio[b]	.15	1.03	.85	.18	1.40	1.04
Change in expenditure (%)	20	23	45	40	57	65
Change in housing quality index (%)	19	24	46	8	34	28
Change in price (%)	2	0	0	29	16	29
Marketwide						
Change in price (%)	1	—2	0	6	—3	3
Change in withdrawals[c]	3	2	4	1	1	2
Change in black population in zone 1[d]	—1	0	—2	0	0	0

[a]"Small Section 8" refers to the proportional allocation type of Section 8 simulations, while "Large Section 8" refers to the fair-share allocation Section 8 simulations. These are defined in chapter 3.
[b]This is the ratio of change in housing expenditures to subsidy.
[c]Change in the number of withdrawals of model dwellings is from a base of 31 in Textile City and 25 in Steel City. Of necessity, the change in withdrawals equals the change in new construction.
[d]Change in the number of black model households in the inner city zone is from a base of five in Textile City and four in Steel City.

The larger income maintenance subsidies are intended to meet many needs other than housing and, indeed, only 15 to 18 percent of the average subsidy is actually spent on improved housing (see the "earmarking" ratio of change in housing expenditure to subsidy in table 10).[2] Under Section 8 programs,

---

[2] Two of the negative income tax experiments have been completed, but figures comparable to our earmarking ratio are yet to be calculated. The

most if not all of the typical subsidy goes to improved housing. Thus, despite the large income maintenance subsidies, people who receive such subsidies do not increase their expenditures on housing as much as people who receive Section 8 payments.

How are the increased housing expenditures divided between quality and higher prices? For the Section 8 programs, improvements in quality are at least as large as, and sometimes larger than, price increases in both Textile City and Steel City. Under the income maintenance program, quality improvements in Steel City are less than a third as large as the price increase, while in Textile City quality improvements are many times larger than the price increase.

Price changes are moderate in both prototype markets under Section 8 because the increased supply resulting from new construction offsets some of the increased demand produced by the subsidies. Because the simulated Section 8 programs allocate half their funds to leasing new units, new construction is as common under Section 8 simulations as under income maintenance, even though the latter program covers more people and pays higher subsidies. Housing improvements under income maintenance come mostly from upgrading existing dwellings. In Steel City, where existing housing is inexpensive to begin with but comparatively expensive to upgrade, large price increases are necessary for this moderate housing improvement. Under the Section 8 programs in Steel City, much more housing improvement is obtained for roughly the same increase in price.

In the Section 8 simulations, the support for new construction causes some owners to withdraw older housing from the market but keeps price changes moderate. Steel City, which grew little during the decade, already had a surplus of modest but adequate dwellings renting at low prices; the emphasis there on new construction under Section 8 results in the substitution of more expensive new units for existing dwellings. In Textile City, however, rapid growth over the decade leaves the market for existing housing tight and prices high; both Section 8 and income maintenance are likely to stimulate new construction there.

"New Jersey" experiment found an increase in home purchases among those eligible for the income subsidy, plus a small effect on the rent of those remaining as renters. The rural experiment also found an increase in home purchases but no effect on those who remained renters. See W. Baumol, *Journal of Human Resources*, vol. 9, no. 2 (1974), pp. 258-260, and *Summary Report: Rural Income Maintenance Experiment* (Washington, D.C.: U.S. Department of Health, Education, and Welfare, November 1976), pp. 60-61.

Program participants would undoubtedly prefer income maintenance to Section 8, primarily because subsidies under the former program are three or four times as large as under the latter program. Another important reason, though (as noted before), is that Section 8 program requirements force some recipients to spend more of their subsidies on housing than they might wish.

Participants must spend enough on housing to make sure that their homes pass program standards in the Section 8 existing program and must pay at least 25 percent of their income for new housing under Section 8 new construction. Many households directed to new units not only have to spend all their subsidies on housing, but also must increase the amounts they previously were allocating to housing from their own incomes. Clearly, recipients will prefer the unrestricted subsidies of the income maintenance program.

Marketwide, neither type of program causes large price changes in either city. The price changes that do occur tend to affect only recipients of program benefits, and there are not enough of these households to have much influence on overall prices. In another market effect, black households show a slight tendency to move out of the core of Textile City under either Section 8 or the income maintenance programs, but there is no movement in Steel City. This difference between cities is due partly to the high cost of inner city housing in Textile City, compared to its cost in Steel City—a phenomenon stemming from Textile City's more rapid population growth and more adaptable housing stock. Another factor accounting for the difference is that some Section 8 housing is assumed to be built outside the inner core of Textile City in the simulations, since one goal of the program is to decentralize low-income households. In the high-minority city, the suburban Section 8 housing is occupied in part by black households.

To summarize, just under 20 percent of the income maintenance subsidies in our simulations go to housing, but this is still enough to cause substantial increases in housing expenditure. The increased expenditure results in improved housing, although in a market with already depressed housing prices and an unresponsive stock, a majority of the increased expenditure goes to higher prices.

In spite of the much smaller Section 8 subsidies, the simulations for that program provide somewhat greater housing improvement for recipients than income maintenance does. This improvement results from the minimum-quality requirements for housing and the steering of recipients to new units. Of course, these restrictions make Section 8 less desirable to the participants. The emphasis on new construction in our Section 8 simulations does have the additional effect of moderating pressures for price increases that both programs create through their subsidies, but that emphasis also leads to more withdrawals. Finally, neither Section 8 nor income maintenance causes large, marketwide price increases, but both increase the number of existing dwellings withdrawn from use.

MORTGAGE INTEREST-RATE REDUCTION

The second program considered in this chapter—a reduction of about 18 percent in the mortgage interest rate for new construction—would stimulate the supply of rather than the demand for housing. This program would reduce the typical interest rate from, for example, 8 percent to 6.5 percent, and would apply to all residential construction during the 1960s, according to our simulations. Moreover, this reduction would cost about the same as the large-scale Section 8 program simulated in the previous chapter.

Housing programs in the past have tended to give much deeper subsidies than this to a limited number of dwellings. The subsidized homeownership and rental-unit building programs resulting from Sections 235 and 236 of the National Housing Act reduced interest rates to 1 percent, while federal subsidies under the public housing program paid 90 percent of mortgage principal and interest. Under all federal programs, however, the number and value of units that could be built have been sharply circumscribed. This will not necessarily be the case for future programs, though, especially if they are intended primarily to stimulate employment in a depressed construction industry rather than to house the poor. An example of such a program—and perhaps the wave of the future—is the 1976 subsidy of $2,000 for the purchase of a new home.

Macroeconomic policies in the past have in fact produced conditions very similar to those created by the interest-rate reduction program we have simulated. The easy money and low interest rates of the 1950s and early 1960s kept the mortgage interest rate substantially lower than its current level, and, of course, those benefits were available for all new construction over that period.

Subsidizing the mortgage interest rate in effect lowers the price for occupying new housing. Because existing units must compete with new ones, the drop in the price of new housing will be reflected in the price for occupying existing housing as well. Middle- and upper-income households will be affected directly because they move into most of the new housing and occupy the existing housing that directly competes with the new. Lower-income households will be affected to the degree that movement into new housing by middle- and upper-income households releases existing dwellings for occupancy by others through the filtering process.

Table 11 compares the effects of the interest subsidy and the large, fair-share Section 8 program in two prototypes, Textile City and Steel City. The comparison depicts the effect on the poorest 20 to 25 percent of the households—the target population in this study—rather than on the direct recipients of either program.

The main effects of the marketwide interest-rate reduction are an increase in new construction and a decrease in the cost of all housing. In Textile City, new construction increases 70 percent and prices drop an average of 7 percent. In Steel City, construction rises by 12 percent and prices drop by 8 percent. Over a decade, as households move from old to new homes, withdrawals of existing units will match the increase in new construction.

Surprisingly, housing consumption marketwide increases negligibly in both cities. Households apparently prefer to use most of their savings from reduced housing costs for other purposes.

The marketwide trends are reflected among the target population, even though none of these poorest of households actually occupies a new dwelling. As a result of middle-income households' transfer to new housing, enough existing units become available to reduce housing costs to the target population even more than to the rest of the market.

As was the case with other households, though, the poor increase their housing consumption little in response to the lower price. In Textile City, the increase is a moderate 8 percent, while the consumption in Steel City actually decreases slightly,

Table 11

COMPARISON OF EFFECTS OF INTEREST-RATE SUBSIDY AND FAIR-SHARE SECTION 8 PROGRAM SIMULATIONS (1960s)

	"Textile City" (Rapid-growth, elastic housing supply)		"Steel City" (Slow-growth, inelastic housing supply)	
	Interest subsidy	Large Section 8	Interest subsidy	Large Section 8
Target population[a]				
Direct subsidy ($)	0	33[b]	0	19[b]
Housing expenditure change (%)	—3	30	—15	43
Housing quantity change (%)	8	30	—3	24
Housing price change (%)	—10	0	—13	15
Change in number moving to new units	0	4	0	2
Marketwide				
Housing price change (%)	—7	0	—8	3
Housing quantity change (%)	2	4	2	2
Change in withdrawals[c] and new construction	5	4	1	2
Change in black population, zone 1[d]	1	—2	1	0

[a]Target population is the 20-25 percent of all households with the lowest incomes.
[b]Subsidies were paid to 70 percent of target population in Textile City and 50 percent in Steel City.
[c]Change in the number of withdrawals of model dwellings is from a base of 31 in Textile City and 25 in Steel City. Of necessity, the change in withdrawals equals the change in new construction.
[d]Change in the number of black model households in the inner city is from a base of five in Textile City and four in Steel City.

—3 percent.[3] Thus, the target population also prefers to transfer savings in housing costs to meet other needs, rather than spend the savings on better housing. This contrasts with results under the Section 8 program which, as noted earlier, induces a large increase in housing consumption among the target population.

---

[3] The reason for the decrease in Steel City is that poor households consume more housing than they want to in the absence of the program. The increased supply of existing dwellings caused by the new construction subsidy enables households to reduce their housing consumption to a more desirable level.

A second contrast in the results of the interest-rate reduction and Section 8 programs is the unevenness of effects in the two markets. In Textile City's fast-growing market with its adaptable existing stock, the interest subsidy produces a large increase in new construction and a moderate improvement in the target population's housing. But in Steel City's slow-growing market with its unresponsive stock of existing dwellings, the interest subsidy causes only a slight increase in new construction and housing for the target population shows no improvement. The amount of new construction and improvements in housing quality are more nearly balanced in both prototype cities under the Section 8 program.

A third contrast between the effects of Section 8 and the interest subsidy is reflected in the figures on who occupies the new housing produced. Both programs emphasize new construction, but the target population occupies none of the new housing built under the interest subsidy, while it occupies most of the new dwellings built as a result of Section 8.

Finally, black households in one prototype area (Textile City) show a slight tendency to move out of the inner city as a result of Section 8, partly because some of the housing under that program was located in other parts of the metropolitan area. That trend is reversed under the mortgage interest subsidy. In that case, a few black households move back into both inner cities and a few whites leave those areas. Apparently, the interest subsidy lowers all prices sufficiently for whites who want to leave the central area to go elsewhere, and for blacks who want to stay or return to do so.

5
URBAN HOUSING
PROJECTIONS FOR 1980

This chapter presents two alternative sets of projections of how well urban families will be housed in 1980. The first set is the "no policy" or base situation, which assumes there will be no new housing programs in the 1970s. The second set of projections assumes the presence of a substantial Section 8 housing program, such as that analyzed in chapter 3. Contrasting the two projections can illuminate the possible effectiveness of Section 8 in alleviating what appear to be adverse housing developments during the 1970s in the absence of this program.

Making these projections with The Urban Institute Model requires the input of 1980 values for a number of important variables. Chief among these are the distribution of household incomes and capital and operating costs for housing. These inputs are only projections for the 1970-80 simulations, whereas values for the 1960-70 simulations come from historical data. Thus, results are necessarily presented here with less confidence than in the previous two chapters.

URBAN HOUSING IN 1980, ASSUMING NO
NEW GOVERNMENT PROGRAMS IN THE 1970s

This section describes urban housing in terms of the progress or deterioration which market forces—income and population growth, inflation in housing prices, and demographic trends—alone produce. This description, then, provides some measure of the need for government action. It also gives guidance on the context of future housing programs by developing information on the amount of housing available at various quality levels in 1980 and the amounts built or withdrawn from the active stock during the seventies.

The need for a projection of the 1980 housing situation of all households—especially those with low-to-moderate incomes —seems particularly urgent in light of developments during the early 1970s. The improvement during the 1960s in the quality of housing occupied by the urban poor has been documented; at the same time, most Americans were devoting a smaller share of their income to housing than during the previous 10 years.[1] Is this progress to be disrupted?

In 1976, household purchasing power was actually less than that between 1970 and 1974, because of extremely high rates of inflation and a stagnant national economy. Operating prices such as utility and home repair costs increased more rapidly than average consumer prices. Obviously, forecasts for the remainder of the decade must be considered, but already the trends just noted and the sharp drop in new residential construction during 1974 to 1976 are expected to leave their mark on the urban housing scene for years to come.

Assumptions Underlying Projections

Differences in the housing situations of urban families in 1970 and 1980 will obviously be affected by basic changes in the characteristics of U.S. families and by economywide cost trends that impinge on housing markets and are therefore determined outside of The Urban Institute's Housing Market Simulation Model. In particular, the values of three inputs must be provided to the model: the 1980 income distribution of each household type, the demographic mix of households in 1980, and the average price of capital and operating inputs over the decade.

The figures in table 12 highlight the major differences in these market forces between 1960 and 1980. They are based on projections, detailed in appendix C, that use a variety of data sources and techniques. Overall, table 12 shows the following:

1. The rise in the price of capital and operating inputs for the production of housing services far exceeds the in-

---

[1] See pages 119-32 of deLeeuw, Schnare, and Struyk, "Housing," in Gorham and Glazer, eds., *The Urban Predicament* (Washington, D.C.: The Urban Institute, 1976).

Table 12

CHANGES IN FACTORS AFFECTING HOUSING MARKETS, 1970–80[a]

A. Composition and Incomes of Model Households, 1970 and 1980

Prototype SMSAs with High-Minority Populations

	Rapid-growth		Slow-growth	
	1970	1980	1970	1980
1. Distribution of model households by household type (%)				
White nonelderly families	58	50	58	49
White elderly families and individuals	23	25	21	24
Black nonelderly families	15	20	15	21
Black elderly families and individuals	5	5	6	6
2. Mean income of model households by household type ($)				
White nonelderly families	13,006	25,307	13,006	25,307
White elderly families and individuals	6,657	15,337	6,657	15,337
Black nonelderly families	8,265	16,871	8,265	16,871
Black elderly families and individuals	4,547	9,376	4,547	9,376

B. Average National Change in Factor Prices and Incomes, 1960-70 and 1970-80

	1960-70	1970-80
1. Change in the price of inputs for producing housing services		
Capital inputs	68	76
Operating inputs	46	119
2. Change in average household income		
Current dollars	66	99
Constant dollars	26	17
3. Change in the Consumer Price Index	40	80

[a]Detailed explanations of the figures in this table are in appendix A.

crease in the Consumer Price Index in both decades. In the 1960s, the price rise of capital inputs surpassed that of operating inputs; in the 1970s the opposite will be the case. Also, during the 1970s the overall increase in the price of housing inputs will be nearly double that of the 1960s.

2. Average household incomes in the 1970s will rise by 17 percent, correcting for inflation. This is down from the 26 percent increase in the 1960s. In current dollars, on the other hand, average incomes will double over the seventies, compared with a 66 percent jump in the 1960s.

3. The shift toward the elderly and single-person households will continue in the 1970s. In addition, in the high-

minority cities, blacks will account for about 25 percent of all households in 1980, compared to 20 percent in 1970. One effect of these changes will be to reduce the share of all white nonelderly households from 58 percent in 1970 to 50 percent in 1980.

4. The divergence in growth rates between the cities classified in 1970 as growing slowly or rapidly over the 1960s will be reduced somewhat in the 1970s, as some rapidly growing cities reduce their growth rates and slowly growing areas increase theirs. In terms of total numbers of households, the rapidly growing areas will experience a 13 percent increase in 1970-80, compared with a 25 percent increase in 1960-70; for the slow growth areas there will be little change in 1970-80 from the 8 percent increase of the 1960s.[2]

These four statements mean that there will be a reduced rate of real income growth; an increase in the relative as well as absolute price of housing; and a shift in the composition of households to those types which have low average incomes but traditionally have devoted a larger share of their incomes to housing than other groups have.

Overall, one would clearly expect reduced demand for the very large units and increased demand for smaller dwellings. Further, because a substantial majority of the units providing low-to-moderate levels of services in 1980 will be those in the 1970 stock, a reduction in the rate at which older housing is retired is also anticipated.

Much less clear is how housing expenditures will be divided between the quantity of services consumed and the price of those services, or whether the division will be the same across income classes and/or household types. It is in this area and in quantifying qualitative assessments of expected change that the model's projections should be most enlightening.

Of equal importance to changes in these exogenous, or external, variables are possible changes in the behavior of producers and consumers over the period for which the projections are made. For most aspects of behavior embodied in the model, there is no simple way to determine whether changes are underway. However, for one of the model's parameters—the

---

[2] For reasons outlined in appendix C, the convergence in model simulation results over the two decades will be somewhat greater than that of the figures just noted.

proportion of income that households would ideally like to spend on shelter—relatively current information is available.

An examination of the income proportion actually spent over an extended period is quite revealing. The ratio declined between 1950 and 1970 for nearly all of those in a group of narrowly defined household types (e.g., nonelderly white households). For all household types combined, though, there was little change because of the shift of households from those with low average income proportions (e.g., nonelderly white households) to those with higher average proportions (elderly or single white households). Over the 1970-73 period, by contrast, there was a fairly sharp upturn in the overall proportion.[3] Hence, at least in the short run, households have been willing to increase housing expenditures as a fraction of income to maintain their housing standards.

It seems likely that this shift is not transitory, given the fact that it applies to rental as well as owner-occupied units, because rental occupants could presumably shift quickly to lower-quality shelter. Thus, the income proportions that households would ideally like to spend on housing—the prespecified housing expense-to-income ratios—have been adjusted upward for the full 1980 simulations.[4]

As noted before, we have no basis for determining whether other shifts in behavior are occurring in the present decade. Of special importance are potential changes in the behavior of housing producers using the existing stock. One could argue that their expectations might be significantly altered by the increased demand for existing rather than new housing, and that improved producer expectations would lead to a greater output at every price. One can readily imagine homeowners deciding to improve

---

[3] The 1970-73 data are from G. Sternlieb, R. W. Burchell, and L. Listokin, *The Private Sector's Role in the Provision of Reasonably Priced Housing* (New Brunswick, N.J.: Rutgers University Center for Urban Policy Research, 1975). The 1950-70 pattern is documented in deLeeuw, Schnare, and Struyk, "Housing."

[4] The housing expense-to-income ratio for four household types was increased 20 percent, consistent with an assumption that a constant quality standard would be maintained within each household type, based on recent experience. The 1970 and 1980 ratios are:

Household Type	Housing expense-to-income ratio	
	1970	1980
White nonelderly families	.18	.22
White individuals and elderly families	.26	.31
Black nonelderly families	.19	.23
Black individuals and elderly families	.27	.32

their units instead of buying a new home.[5] On the other hand, the increased number of communities imposing rent controls and the reduction in certain tax advantages to owners of rental housing clearly work to reduce expected returns.

Overall producer expectations may be shifting, but there is no reliable way to tell. Without the requisite information, it has been assumed here that supplier behavior during the 1970s will be identical with that in the 1960s.

Simulation Results

In examining the housing situation in 1980, two factors are emphasized here: (1) the level of housing consumption and the proportion of income actually devoted to housing by various groups of households, and (2) usage rates in 1980 for the stock of housing existing in 1970. For the first factor, the amount of service and the prices per unit of service are given for households in each income quartile for each decade. In addition, the percentage of households in each of the four household types living in substandard housing is computed.

The "standard dwelling" in these computations is one having more than the minimum number of services required to meet the standards for participation in a large-scale national housing allowance program in 1970, had such a program been in effect.[6] To put this standard in perspective, note that it is somewhat below what is required for new units by local building codes.

There are also figures here on (1) the ratios of housing expense to income for each income quartile and (2) the composition of the housing stock at the end of the decade in terms of new and existing units. (For reference, the mean and range of the 1970 household incomes in the four income quartiles are shown in table 13.)

The basic results of the 1970-80 simulations are presented

---

[5] On this point see F. James, *Back to the City: An Appraisal of Housing Reinvestment and Population Change in Urban America*, (Paper 241-3. 1977, The Urban Institute, Washington, D.C.).

[6] This refers to a type of "housing gap" allowance program in which 22 percent of households are eligible for participation. The allowance payment to a household is determined by the formula: $S = C^* - bY$. S is the payment allowed. C^* is the maximum payment and is sufficient to provide a no-income household with standard housing. Y is household income, and b is the tax rate, at which S is reduced by an increment to income.

Other definitions of C^* are possible in the gap formulation, but the minimum standard unit has been used in the reference program. Separate C^*s are used for nonelderly families on the one hand and elderly families and individuals on the other. This allowance program is the main one reported in chapter 6 of this volume.

Table 13
1970 HOUSEHOLD INCOME QUARTILES FOR HIGH-MINORITY PROTOTYPE CITIES

	Income Quartile			
	Lowest	Second	Third	Highest
Rapid-growth				
Mean	$2,612	$6,894	$11,089	$21,190
Range				
Lowest	1,003	4,784	8,760	14,194
Highest	4,707	8,343	13,505	40,094
Slow-growth				
Mean	2,563	6,676	11,088	21,236
Range				
Lowest	1,118	4,723	8,998	14,816
Highest	4,559	8,215	13,940	37,939

in table 14. As noted in chapter 2, these simulations have only been done for the two prototype cities with large minority populations (Textile and Steel). This choice is based on the greater diversity of results between city types associated with growth rates than with racial composition. Also, it will be recalled that developing the high-minority prototype cities involved using the same 1960 housing stock but different growth rates in low-to-moderate income households for the slowly and rapidly growing cities. Thus, the 1960 situation is the same for both types of cities (during 1960-70); the first figure column in table 14 indicates the 1960 or basic housing situation.

Because housing conditions in 1960 are based on historical, or census, data, the division of housing expenditures between the price per unit of service and the quantity of housing services is not known. (The model makes this separation for the 1970 and 1980 results.) For the present computations, the price per unit of service is assumed to be the same throughout the market at a value of $1.00 in 1960. Thus, all the 1960 prices in entry 2 of table 14 are the same. This particular assumption implies a strong demand for comparatively low-quality units in 1960, an assumption consistent with several empirical studies.[7]

---

[7] These studies mainly focus on the price paid by black households for housing compared with that paid by white households in the same markets. The studies show a very tight market in the early 1960s (i.e., blacks paying more) and a much looser situation by 1970 (i.e., blacks paying the same or less). For a review of this work, see A. Schnare and R. Struyk, "An Analysis of Ghetto Housing Prices Over Time."

Table 14
HOUSING IN HIGH-MINORITY METROPOLITAN AREAS, 1980

Housing Indicator	All High-Minority, 1960	Textile — High-growth, inelastic[a]				Steel — Slow-growth, elastic[a]				Steel — Slow-growth, inelastic[a]			
		1970	1980	Percentage Change 1960-70	Percentage Change 1970-80	1970	1980	Percentage Change 1960-70	Percentage Change 1970-80	1970	1980	Percentage Change 1960-70	Percentage Change 1970-80
1. Average quantity of housing services													
Lowest income quartile	43	58	60	35	3	59	66	37	12	59	65	37	10
Second income quartile	77	96	108	25	13	96	112	25	17	96	112	25	17
Third income quartile	105	140	170	33	21	135	165	29	22	136	168	30	24
Highest income quartile	167	208	231	25	11	216	232	29	7	205	231	23	13
2. Average price of housing services[b]													
Lowest income quartile	1.00	1.02	2.32	2	127	1.10	2.59	10	135	.83	2.02	-17	143
Second income quartile	1.00	1.24	2.58	24	108	1.21	2.61	21	116	1.20	2.44	20	103
Third income quartile	1.00	1.24	2.73	24	120	1.24	2.73	24	120	1.24	2.67	24	115
Highest income quartile	1.00	1.24	2.77	24	123	1.22	2.76	22	126	1.23	2.75	23	124
3. Average housing expense-to-income ratio[c]													
Lowest income quartile	.22	.28	.39	27	39	.30	.47	36	57	.23	.36	5	57
Second income quartile	.20	.21	.27	5	29	.21	.30	5	43	.20	.26	0	30
Third income quartile	.19	.18	.23	-5	28	.18	.22	-5	22	.18	.22	-5	22
Highest income quartile	.19	.15	.19	-21	27	.15	.19	-21	27	.14	.19	-26	36

4. Percentage of model households in substandard housing[a]

	(1)	(2)	(3)	(4)	(5)	(6)	(7)	(8)	(9)	(10)	(11)	(12)	(13)
White													
Nonelderly families	15	9	9	−10	0	5	5	−67	0	5	5	−67	0
Individual and elderly family	57	22	8	−41	−64	14	11	−75	−21	14	11	−75	−27
Black[e]													
Nonelderly families	67	17	22	−75	23	20	29	−70	45	0	14	−100	[f]
Individual and elderly family	0	—	50	0	[f]	—	50	—	[f]	0	50	—	[f]
5. Household and dwellings													
a. No. of households	40	40	46			33	36			33	36		
b. No. of new units	12	12	7			5	3			8	6		
c. No. of units[g]													
i. Start-of-decade	31	31	40			31	33			31	33		
ii. Start-of-decade units occupied at end of decade	28	28	39			28	33			25	30		

[a] Differences in the elasticity of supply are differences in how producers using the stock of housing present at the start of the simulation period respond to changes in the price offered them by consumers. In the elastic case, this responsiveness is 1.4 times that of the inelastic case.

[b] The price per unit of service in 1960 is $1.00; for a new unit over the decade of the 1960s, $1.24; over the decade of the 1970s, $2.78.

[c] Household incomes are exogenous to the model but the housing expenses of the individual households are determined as part of the model solution.

[d] The minimum quantity of services for a unit classified as "standard" is equivalent to that which a household must have consumed to be eligible for participation in a national housing allowance program in 1970. Separate quantities are defined for (a) nonelderly families and (b) elderly families and single individuals.

[e] The numbers in these rows should be viewed with caution because of the small number of black model households in the cities.

[f] Not defined.

[g] The difference between i and ii is the number of dwellings withdrawn from the stock over the decade.

To the right of the results for 1960 are columns of information on Textile and Steel Cities under each assumption about producer responsiveness—i.e., the standard elastic and inelastic distinctions for the two areas. The 1970 and 1980 housing situations are described in terms of both the *level* of consumption, housing prices, and other factors and the *percentage change* in these factors over the two decades.[8]

Turning first to the change in the quantity of housing consumed between 1960-70 and 1970-80, entry 1 in table 14 shows that even with the assumed increased expenditure on housing, there will be deterioration—compared to the progress of the 1960s. Note, however, that the housing situation of all groups improves over the decade, albeit at a slower rate than in the 1960s. The decline in growth appears to be sharper in the rapidly growing Textile City under the inelastic supply assumption than in the parallel slow-growing situation in Steel City. This might be expected because there was substantially less underutilized stock in the fast-growing city in 1970.

The role of increased prices relative to real income growth is evident, particularly in the prices paid by those in the lowest income quartile. For these households, new units, with their high minimum requirements, are prohibitively expensive. Over the 1960s, low-income households generally faced little increase in the price per unit of housing services; the maximum increase was 10 percent in Textile City. This lack of increase was due mainly to the large amount of new construction for other households, made possible by the combination of favorable capital cost conditions and the substantial growth of real income. Reduced immigration to many cities at the end of the decade simultaneously decreased demand for lower-quality housing. Thus, the supply of such units was increasing in the face of declining demand.

The 1970s show a strong revival in the demand for smaller units in response to higher prices and increased numbers of households with modest incomes—the latter resulting from changes in household composition. Note that the demand will be for existing units providing low levels of housing services. The result will be price pressure for smaller units: Where discounts are great, the pressure will be great, since prices can rise con-

---

[8] Note that no results are presented for the rapidly growing, elastic case. Solutions which met the standard criteria for this case were not obtainable, as it would have been necessary to assign two high- and moderate-income households to new units.

siderably before they compete with other units. Steel City, under the inelastic supply assumption, provides a dramatic case of this phenomenon, as prices rise from a substantial discount in 1970.

The effect of high prices is also demonstrated in the pattern of utilization of the initial-year housing stock at the end of the respective decades. Over the 1960-70 period, both prototype cities retired at least 10 percent of their 1960 dwellings from the stock (the difference between entries 5ci and 5cii in table 14), with the slow-growing city under the inelastic supply assumption retiring the largest share.

For 1970-80, however, the rate of retirements will fall sharply as a greater demand for existing units will be spurred by the high price of new units. In the Steel City case, no initial-year dwellings will be retired, and in the Textile City inelastic case, only about 2 percent of the 1970 stock will drop out. However, in the Steel City inelastic case, about 7 percent of the stock will still be retired. Overall, then, sharp reductions in housing abandonments and in low vacancy rates are expected generally in 1980 compared with 1970, but in some markets these problems may continue.

While the points just made establish the general picture, care must be taken to sort through some of the patterns being observed. In particular, reduced improvement in housing quality for those in the lowest income quartiles in both cities is caused not only by the general shift in housing prices relative to incomes, but also by the increase in the number of lower-income household types such as elderly and single persons.

The figures in entry 4 of table 14 are designed to show what happens to individual types of households. In addition, by measuring their progress in housing improvement relative to a minimum requirement for standard dwellings, one can observe the degree to which households will be forced below this standard by 1980 because of economic conditions. For example, the pattern for the two types of white households is quite clear: There will be a decline in the rate of households moving into standard-quality housing, but there will be no increase in the number of households in substandard units. In other words, the gains of the past will not be lost.

The results for the two types of black households must be interpreted with considerably more caution. Because of the small number of black model households (two elderly families or single individuals and four to nine nonelderly families) a change in a single model household can overstate what might actually be happening. This "discreteness" problem is evident for the 1960 results, which show no black elderly families or single individuals living in substandard units. Looking at the results for blacks as a whole, it appears that more blacks could be living in substandard housing in 1980 than in 1970 unless they are willing to devote an even higher proportion of their incomes to housing than has been assumed.

Lastly, in terms of how much income is spent on housing (entry 3), the results of the simulations for the 1970-80 period show substantial increases in the ratios of housing expense to income for all income quartiles. This finding is logical, given the 10 percent increase in the parameter reflecting a household's ideal ratio of housing expenses to income. The distribution of the rise in the ratio by income level, though, is not preordained. As with the pattern of increases observed for the 1960s, the lowest income group experiences the largest increase in the ratio of housing expense to income. This increase of about 40 percent for the poor is caused by the increased competition for smaller dwellings. The ratios of the rich also rise a good deal because of the jump in the price per unit of service of new dwellings.

The picture for the 1970s, then, is not so bright as that for the sixties. While most households will be better housed in 1980 than they were in 1970, the rate of improvement will be seriously diminished. Among urban blacks, there is the distinct possibility that more will live in substandard dwellings in 1980 than in 1970. Households of all income levels will be devoting a greater share of their incomes to housing. People living in cities that grew more rapidly than the national norm during the 1960s (and hence entered the 1970s with tight housing market conditions) will see their housing situations improve less than that of people in the slower-growing areas where a larger proportion of the 1970 stock is not fully used.

Preliminary Assessment

The results just reviewed indicate fairly sharp shifts in the housing situation in 1980, compared to 1970. The credibility of these findings depends on how well the exogenous inputs have been predicted for 1980 and on the functioning of the model itself. Besides reviewing these factors, however, it was possible at the end of 1976 to compare the full set of predictions with data from the first few years of the decade. It will be seen, though, that mainly because of ignorance about the timing of various behavioral responses, it was difficult to make a very definitive comparison.

Three types of data were available in 1976 for comparative purposes: those on housing quality; maintenance and improvement expenditures for existing units; and the rate of appreciation of owner-occupied houses, plus the rents of rental properties. Some summary figures on each of these factors are given in the three parts of table 15 for the 1970-74 period.

Part A of the table provides a number of conventional measures of the amount and quality of housing used by those living within metropolitan areas. These data, drawn from U.S. Census Bureau studies, indicate a steady increase in the average quality of housing between 1970 and 1974. Interestingly, there has been little change in the distribution of dwellings by the number of rooms or bedrooms, which are useful proxies for size. Any attempt at a precise comparison of the rate of improvement in these quality indicators over 1970-74 with that over the 1960s is fraught with problems. Those problems include lack of available data and incomparability in definitions of the areas included. Nevertheless, the two trends are roughly comparable.

On the other hand, the part B figures on percentage changes in maintenance expenditures by owner-occupants and landlords between 1968 and 1974 show a sharp downturn in the 1970s, after those figures are deflated for price increases.[9] For owner-occupied units, the reduction occurred at the beginning of the decade, while for rental properties the shift happened after 1972. The point, however, is that with these expenditures holding essentially constant, the main source of improvement in housing quality will be the addition of new units to the stock and the withdrawal of the worst existing dwellings.

The evidence on consumption and investment, on balance, does not paint a clear picture, although some improvement is consistent with the predictions made. In fact, a sharp improvement in the early 1970s would not necessarily be incompatible with the predictions. There is a general consensus that housing consumption decisions are based on normal or long-run income, and this consensus is built into the model. No reliable information has been developed on the length of time required for families to revise prior estimates of their normal income. In other words, most households may have been using the income expecta-

---

[9] This data series was only begun in 1968; thus, longer-term comparisons are not possible.

tions they had in the late 1960s to guide their housing consumption in the early 1970s.

This finding would be especially true if the inflation and recession associated with the recent oil embargo and grain

Table 15

INDICATORS OF TRENDS IN HOUSING QUALITY AND PRICES IN THE EARLY 1970s

A. Selected Physical Attributes of Dwellings in SMSAs[a]

Attribute	Percentage by Year		
	1970	1973	1974
1. Number of rooms			
1-2	6%	5%	5%
3-4	32	32	32
5-6	44	44	44
7 or more	17	18	18
2. Number of bedrooms			
None	3	3	3
1	18	17	17
2	33	32	33
3 or more	47	48	47
3. Number of bathrooms			
1	} 77	64	62
1 and ½		12	13
2 or more	18	21	22
None or shared	4	3	2
4. Heating equipment			
Central system	74	79	80
Other	26	21	20
5. Units with air conditioning			
Central system	27	31	31
Window units	12	19	21
6. Units with following:			
a. Interior walls and ceilings that have:			
i. Open cracks or holes			
Owner-occupied	[b]	3	3
Renter-occupied	[b]	11	10
ii. Broken plaster or peeling paint			
Owner-occupied	[b]	2	2
Renter-occupied	[b]	9	8
b. Interior floor with holes			
Owner-occupied	[b]	1	1
Renter-occupied	[b]	3	3
c. Roof leakage			
Owner-occupied	[b]	5	4
Renter-occupied	[b]	9	8
d. Exposed electrical wiring			
Owner-occupied	[b]	3	2
Renter-occupied	[b]	4	3
e. Auxiliary heaters used because of poor heating			
Owner-occupied	[b]	7	6
Renter-occupied	[b]	15	15

Table 15 (continued)
B. Trends in Maintenance and Investment Expenditures on Residential Properties[c] (percentage increases)

Tenure, dwelling type	1968-70	1970-72	1972-74
One-unit, owner-occupied			
Increase in current dollars	55	18	22
Increase in constant dollars	39	5	1
Rental properties			
Increase in current dollars	16	25	17
Increase in constant dollars	4	12	−3

C. Changes in Housing Rents and House Values, 1970-1974[d]

	Percentage change, 1970-73		Percentage change, 1973-74	
	Central Cities	Suburbs	Central Cities	Suburbs
Median value of owner-occupied units	36	42	11	10
Median gross rents of rental units	22	25	8	6

[a]Figures are taken from U.S. Bureau of the Census, *Annual Housing Survey*, part A, "General Housing Characteristics," and part B, "Indicators of Housing and Neighborhood Quality," H-150-7nA and H-150-7nB Series (Washington, D.C.: U.S. Government Printing Office, 1973 and 1974).
[b]Data are not available for 1970.
[c]Figures are taken from U.S. Bureau of the Census, *Residential Alterations and Repairs*, C50 Series, various issues (Washington, D.C.: Government Printing Office). Current dollar amounts in the C50 Series were deflated with the construction price index of the Department of Commerce to obtain the constant dollar figures.
[d]See F. James, "Housing Reinvestment and the Central City: The Future of Older Urban Housing" (Washington, D.C.: Urban Institute Working Paper 241-02, 1976).

shortages were viewed at the time as extraordinary events. With expectations just being revised, say, in 1974-75, the main impact on housing trends will show up in the years immediately ahead.

The final pieces of information to be mustered are the average rates of appreciation of owner-occupied housing and the rates of rental increase for dwellings with different ages and locations. These comparisons are fairly crude: They assume that older dwellings and those in central cities provide a smaller quantity of housing services than their newer or suburban counterparts. These data, shown in part C of table 15, indicate that the 1970-73 pattern is similar to the one observed over the 1960s for newer and suburban properties that had higher rates of rental increase or property appreciation than others.

For 1973-74, the pattern reverses itself, with older and central city dwellings doing better. This pattern is consistent with the time lag required before the price pressures from the high costs of new dwellings work themselves through the market. In addition, one study shows that expenditures on maintaining and improving existing units have been differentially greater for older and central city units.[10] While it is clearly too early to assert that these data confirm anything about the model's predictions, the figures do demonstrate some plausibility in those projections.

SECTION 8 IN THE 1970s

Against the background of a 1980 housing situation without major government initiatives, the potential importance of Section 8 in further improving the housing quality or lowering the rent burden of the poor is obvious. The Section 8 program reviewed here is similar to that explored in considerable detail in chapter 3. In particular, a program leasing half-new and half-existing units was simulated for Textile and Steel Cities, under the assumption of inelastic supplier response. The simulated program involves the same number of households as did the 1960-70 Section 8 program under the fair-share allocation in these cities. The 1970 fair market rents are boosted to reflect estimated increases in the price of housing services over the 1970s; income eligibility limits are increased similarly. On the other hand, minimum housing standards for participation and general eligibility criteria are the same as those used in chapter 3.

Several events over the 1970s could alter the effectiveness of this program, compared with the results reviewed for the 1960s. A major factor is the steep rise in the price of housing services to the poor in the absence of the program. This rise largely accounts for the increase in the rent burden of the poor. Since most low-income people would be devoting well over 25 percent of their incomes to housing, participation in the Section 8 program should increase. A major effect of the program should be reductions in the ratios of housing expenditure to income for poor households.

At the same time, urban households were generally better housed in 1970 than in 1960. Among those moderate-income households eligible for Section 8 participation, some may have

---

[10] F. James, "Housing Reinvestment and the Older Central City: The Future of Older Urban Housing" (Washington, D.C.: Urban Institute Working Paper 241-02, 1976).

increased their housing consumption beyond the limits imposed by the FMRs. Even though this high standard has been achieved only by devoting more than a quarter of their income to housing, these households may elect to live in the more expensive dwellings rather than participate in the program.

The results of the simulations, presented in table 16, are for households divided by income quartiles. Eligible households are concentrated in the lowest quartile, although a few are in the second quartile. Looking first at participation rates, one sees that full participation has occurred.[11] This is in contrast to the .83 and .75 participation rates for Textile and Steel Cities, respectively, under a similar program in 1970.[12] The difference is that the price of low-quality housing rises substantially between 1970 and 1980; thus, by 1980 low-income households can no longer find bargain prices in substandard housing and will turn to the program for relief from their rising housing expenses.

Housing consumption rises for the lowest income quartile by about 10 percent under the program (entry 4 in table 16), and the increase for participating households is about the same. Increases for the two lower income quartiles are produced by the combination of direct increases by participants and other increases made possible by the program's market effects. Consumption by nonparticipants increases more in Textile City because (1) the construction of new units under Section 8 produces a slight loosening of initially tight market conditions, and (2) prices faced by the poor do not rise by quite as much over the decade.

In Steel City, new construction does not produce this favorable price effect. Here the initial price level is much lower (relative to the price per unit of service for new construction, which is the same in both cities). Thus, some existing dwellings are producing few housing services at the time the program is introduced. The prices of these units must rise if the dwellings are to improve enough to meet program standards. Competition among participants is sufficient to do this, except in the case of the lowest-quality unit, which no household chooses and which is therefore withdrawn from the stock.

---

[11] Recall from chapter 3 that in most of the simulations, some eligible households were assigned to new units. This is the equivalent of having local housing authorities steer households since, in a framework stressing utility, new units would not have been chosen under the 1960-70 conditions. This point has not been investigated.

[12] For the 1970 results see appendix D, table D-2, columns C14 and C16.

Table 16

EFFECTS OF MAJOR SECTION 8 PROGRAM IN HIGH-MINORITY CITIES, 1980[a]

	Textile City, Rapid-Growth			Steel City, Slow-Growth		
	Without Section 8	With Section 8	Percentage change	Without Section 8	With Section 8	Percentage change
1. Participation rate	—	1.00	—	—	1.00	—
2. Average subsidy	—	$50	—	—	$76	—
3. Earmarking ratio[b]	—	.57	—	—	.91	—
4. Average quantity of housing services						
Lowest income quartile	60	65	8	65	72	11
Second income quartile	108	119	10	112	113	1
Third income quartile	170	166	−2	168	162	−4
Highest income quartile	231	233	1	231	229	−1
5. Average price per unit of housing services						
Lowest income quartile	2.32	2.15	7	2.02	2.14	6
Second income quartile	2.58	2.60	1	2.44	2.57	5
Third income quartile	2.73	2.73	0	2.67	2.68	0
Highest income quartile	2.77	2.77	0	2.75	2.75	0
6. Average housing expense-to-income ratio						
Lowest income quartile	.39	.31	−21	.36	.33	−8
Second income quartile	.27	.25	−7	.26	.23	−12
Third income quartile	.20	.19	−5	.20	.19	−5
Highest income quartile	.19	.20	5	.19	.20	5
7. Number of model dwellings present in 1970 withdrawn by 1980	1	6	—	0	5	—
8. Number of model dwellings built 1970-80	7	12	—	3	8	—

[a]The Section 8 program is that described in chapter 3 as using a mix of 50 percent new construction and 50 percent existing housing, with the number of eligible households determined by the fair-share allocation. For Textile City, the results are for a 60 percent new, 40 percent existing unit mix (see text for explanation). All results in the table are based on the assumption of a relatively inelastic response to changes in demand by suppliers, using the existing housing stock.

[b]The earmarking ratio is defined as the dollar change in housing expenditure over the cost of the subsidy. It is defined only for par-

The result in Steel City is the seemingly paradoxical outcome of increases in consumption and in the price per unit of housing services—indicating the importance of the implicit income gains by participants and the marketwide program effects. An additional effect of this combination is a higher earmarking ratio in Steel City than in Textile City.

Turn next to the ratio of housing expenditures to income. The table shows declines in the housing cost burden for all low-income households in both cities. These declines result from even larger declines achieved by program participants. Without the Section 8 program, participants would devote 31 percent of their income to housing in Textile City and 38 percent in Steel City. With Section 8 in effect, these figures drop to the 25 percent mandated by the program. Hence, in Textile City the average rent burden drops by 19 percent and in Steel City by 34 percent. These represent major improvements in the welfare of participants not reflected elsewhere in the results.[13]

One final point must be raised, though its implications are tentative. The Section 8 program reported for Textile City in 1980 has a 60-40 percentage split between new and existing housing, rather than the standard 50/50 mix. The reason is that under the 50/50 mix, the model could not find a suitable allocation of Section 8 participants for the available existing units. When some participants were transferred from the existing to the new side of the program, a suitable allocation was found. This suggests that sufficient amounts of new construction may not be forthcoming from the private sector, even in rapidly growing cities, under a large Section 8 existing program.

The implication here contrasts with our findings for 1960-70, where additional new construction seems adequate to meet the needs of subsidy recipients in rapidly growing cities (See chapters 3 and 6). The difference between 1970 and 1980 may be based on the large increase in new construction prices over the decade and the accompanying decline in amounts of new construction at all quality levels in the absence of any subsidy program. However, there has been too little exploration of Section 8 for

---

[13] This phenomenon has been observed in early experience with the Section 8 program. Under certain set-aside provisions, Section 8 subsidies are given to households living in FHA-insured (often government-subsidized) projects potentially in danger of default. The main effect on tenants of these projects, at least in the short term, has been the reduction in rent burden. For details, see *Section 8 Housing Assistance Payments Program: The Loan-Management Set-Aside* (Washington, D.C.: Office of Assistant Secretary for Policy Development and Research, HUD, 1977).

1980 to draw a firm conclusion about the adequacy of new construction provided by the private market under a large Section 8 program in a rapidly growing area.

Overall, these simulations are certainly too few to allow firm conclusions; still, three general observations seem warranted. First, even a large-scale Section 8 program will, in general, cause only small market disruptions. Second, Section 8 will cause a modest increase in the housing consumption of participants and, under some market conditions, of nonparticipants as well. Third, a major effect will be a reduction in the housing burden of participants, an effect that could be achieved through other types of cash transfers.

6
WHICH HOUSING POLICY IS BEST?[1]

The answer to that question has been the theme of this book. That answer is: It depends. It depends on which objectives are weighted most heavily; on conditions in the housing market at the time a program is introduced; and on income trends, growth in the number of households, and the cost of producing housing. There is no single answer; indeed, there may not even be a single answer for each metropolitan area.

No attempt is made here to define the "best" policy. Rather, a contrast is made of the long-term effects of a large number of alternative policies on how well people are housed and the condition of the housing stock under different market conditions. The procedure in this chapter contrasts with that in the previous chapters, where the effects of a single program are compared across cities. Here the effects of alternative policies in the same market are contrasted and then compared with the effects of the same set of policies in another type of market. An illustration of the question addressed here is: Which policies are more effective in rapidly growing cities? In earlier chapters the question was, for example: What are the effects of the Section 8 program in different cities?

The purpose of this chapter, then, is to draw conclusions about the effects of alternative programs under different market

---

[1] With Michael S. Owen.

conditions. Thus, this section is a summary of results from the previous chapters. Unlike most summaries, though, this one introduces several new programs for consideration. This will ensure that the conclusions drawn are based on a broad spectrum of potential housing programs.

More specifically, the effects of 10 housing programs in two of the prototype cities are examined. The two locales are (1) Textile City, the high-minority area with a fast-growing, low-to-moderate income population, and (2) Grain City, the low-minority area with a slow-growing, low-to-moderate income population. These cities represent two extremes out of the four prototype cities and should provide a sharp contrast. For Textile City, one assumes relatively high elasticity or supplier response to demand changes in the existing housing stock. In Grain City, the inelastic assumption is used, a divergence that heightens the contrast between the two areas. Results of simulations in these two divergent markets should span the range likely in most cities.

The programs considered here include those discussed in detail in prior chapters: Section 8, a construction subsidy for all new units, and major welfare reform, plus the following additions:

- Housing allowance combined with new construction subsidy;
- Housing allowance combined with rehabilitation subsidy;
- Small-scale welfare reform;
- Public housing;
- Targeted new construction subsidy (aimed only at certain types of dwellings).

There are clear limitations to the analysis in this chapter. Only results for some types of cities are included. More importantly, some of the programs themselves are not strictly comparable; they differ in aggregate cost, coverage, and how they work. Further, any comparative analysis of housing programs is plagued by the multiple objectives these programs attempt to serve. Finally, a single, comprehensive measure of program benefits has proved to be infeasible to calculate.[2] This means that in comparing program effects, one must consider a fairly large

---

[2] For a full discussion of the problems in constructing a comprehensive benefit-cost measure, see L. Ozanne, "Calculating Benefit-Cost Ratios with The Urban Institute Model" (Washington, D.C.: Urban Institute Working Paper 235-3, 1977).

number of indicators. These shortcomings notwithstanding, the comparisons here permit broad conclusions about program effectiveness.

THE PROGRAMS

A concise summary of the 10 programs included in this analysis is in table 17. Only four types of programs among the 10 have not been treated at length elsewhere in this volume:

Table 17

SUMMARY COMPARISON OF VARIOUS HOUSING PROGRAMS[a]

Type of Program	Program Description[b]	Conditions for Participation
1. Housing allowance	Cash grants to households, earmarked for housing; 22 percent of households eligible. Subsidies determined under "housing gap" formula: $S = C^* - bY$ where C^* is cost of dwelling, Y is household income, and b is tax rate or household contribution rate (set at .2 in these simulations).	Income test: $Y \leq C^*/0.2$. This implies income limits of $5,000 for nonelderly families and $4,000 for elderly families and individuals. Housing consumption requirement: Nonelderly families must occupy dwellings providing at least 65 units of service per month; elderly families and individuals, 54.
2. Small income maintenance program	Unrestricted cash grants to 22 percent of households. Transfer payments determined by housing allowance gap formula.	Income test as above. No minimum housing consumption requirement.
3. Major income maintenance program	Unrestricted cash grants to 27 percent of households. Transfer payments determined as $S = P - 0.6Y$, where P is the maximum payment and equals the 1969 poverty income definition (defined separately for nonelderly families compared to elderly families and individuals). The .6Y term indicates that S is reduced by 60 cents for every dollar of additional income.	Income test: maximum incomes for nonelderly families, $6,250; for elderly families and individuals, $3,300.

Table 17 (continued)

Type of Program	Program Description[b]	Conditions for Participation
4. Across-the-board new construction subsidy	Subsidy (12 percent of the cost of capital) available on all new residential construction.	No special requirements. Unit must meet building codes and, hence, provide at least 65 units of service per month.
5. Targeted, one-step new construction subsidy	Thirteen percent subsidy on capital costs of dwellings providing less than 200 units of service per month. Maximum corresponds roughly to $24,000 a dwelling.	Dwellings must meet minimum standards and provide no more than 200 units of service per month.
6. Targeted, two-step new construction subsidy	Subsidy of 21 percent available to new dwellings providing 65-150 units of service per month, 11 percent for units providing 150-200. Dwellings of 150 units of service cost roughly $18,000.	Only quantity of service requirements noted in program description.
7. Combined housing allowance and one-step new construction subsidy	Small housing allowance, with 11 percent of households eligible. Gap-type program (see 1 above). One-step construction subsidy as described before, except subsidy is 9 percent of capital costs.	Allowance income tests: Income maximums are $2,900 for nonelderly families and $2,050 for elderly families and individuals. Housing consumption requirements: Nonelderly families must consume at least 48 units of housing services per month; elderly families and individuals, 34. Restrictions on supplier subsidy: same as in 5, above.
8. Combined housing allowance and rehabilitation subsidy	Housing allowance program, with 16 percent of households eligible. Gap-type program (see 1 above). Reduces prices paid by landlords of existing housing for capital services to make improvements.	Allowance income limits: nonelderly families, $3,800; elderly families and individuals, $3,000. Housing consumption requirements: Nonelderly families must consume at least 65 units of housing services per month; elderly families and individuals, 54. Depth of capital subsidy to suppliers varies with pre-subsidy housing output, is deepest for units close to quantities required by housing allowance program.

Type of Program	Program Description[b]	Conditions for Participation
9. Section 8 housing assistance	Ten percent of households eligible. Government leases 50 percent new and 50 percent existing dwellings. Household contributes 25 percent of its income.	Income test: Income limits vary with family size and are expressed as functions of local area median income. Consumption/supplier requirements: New dwellings must provide 65 units of service per month; existing, 45. Dwellings must not rent for more than fair market rent established separately for new and existing dwellings.
10. Public housing	Conventional public housing. Enough new units built for 5 percent of population. Household contributes 25 percent of income to live in unit.	Income test: Household income cannot exceed 80-90 percent of Section 8 income limits.

[a]All monetary figures are in 1970 dollars.

[b]More complete descriptions are available as follows: For the 22 percent housing allowance program, small income maintenance program, and across-the-board new construction, see F. deLeeuw and R. Struyk, *The Web of Urban Housing*, chapter 6 (Washington, D.C.: The Urban Institute, 1975). For the one- and two-step new construction programs, with and without housing allowances, see M. Owen and R. Struyk, "Market Effects of New Construction Subsidy-Housing Allowance Programs" (Washington, D.C.: Urban Institute Working Paper 221-4, 1975). For the rehabilitation-allowance combination and related programs, see L. Ozanne, "Housing Allowances in Combination with New Construction and Rehabilitation Subsidies" (Washington, D.C.: Urban Institute Working Paper 221-9, 1975). For the Section 8 program, see chapter 3 of this volume, and for the major income maintenance program, see chapter 4 of this volume.

housing allowances, targeted capital subsidies for new construction, rehabilitation studies, and construction of conventional[3] public housing.

Housing Allowances

A housing allowance is a cash grant given to income-eligible households, provided they live in housing of a certain quality. The particular type of allowance program included here is the "gap" type, in which the cash grant received (S) equals the difference between the monthly rent (C*) of a dwelling meeting

---

[3] "Conventional" means the original type of multiunit, government-built and run housing, rather than the newer variations such as turnkey, leased units, etc. (some of which involve the private sector).

program standards and 20 percent of household income (Y).[4] To receive the grant, a household must occupy housing that at least meets physical standards, although the dwelling may rent for more or less than the C* amount. If it rents for less, the participant is allowed to keep the difference—a significant shopping incentive.

Because of the requirement for standard quality housing, one expects housing demand by program participants to be concentrated just above the program's standard. Such a concentration could cause housing prices per unit of service to rise, unless the supply of suitable housing is increased through other actions.

The national prototype program simulated would make about 22 percent of households income-eligible. Of all the programs included, the housing allowance is the only one for which there are reliable national cost data. It is estimated that in 1976, an allowance program similar to the one used here cost about $7.6 billion in cash transfers and perhaps another $1 billion to administer.[5] This figure serves as a benchmark for measuring the probable costs of other programs.

Targeted Subsidies

The across-the-board new construction subsidy, analyzed in detail in chapter 4 (see row 4 in table 17), is available to all new housing, regardless of its cost or the income of its occupant. In contrast, the one- and two-step construction subsidies (rows 5 and 6 in the table) place restrictions on the size or cost of dwellings qualifying for the subsidy, thereby targeting the program to moderate-income households. The two-step program offers a deep subsidy to new units, such as those qualifying under the Section 235 homeownership assistance program, and a shallow one to larger but still modest new dwellings. All these construction subsidies will tend to cause more new housing to be built and should therefore produce an excess supply of units in the lower-income share of the market.

Rehab Subsidy

The rehabilitation subsidy, combined with a small housing allowance (entry 8), provides a subsidy for capital used in im-

[4] For a general description of alternative housing allowance formulations, see F. de Leeuw, S. H. Leaman, and H. Blank, *The Design of a Housing Allowance* (Washington, D.C.: The Urban Institute, 1970).

[5] R. Sepanik, "Variations of Selective Design Elements for Housing Allowances: Simulations Using the TRIM Model" (Washington, D.C.: Urban Institute Working Paper 216-29, 1975).

proving the dwelling unit. In the particular program used here, the depth of the subsidy varies, depending on the dwelling's level of services, or output, at the beginning of the period studied. The capital price reduction is greatest for dwellings producing 1960 levels of housing service that are near the minimum required for housing allowances; that reduction declines as dwelling size increases. This design works to augment the supply of allowance-acceptable units in the critical range, and thus should offset inflationary pressures caused by the allowances. No current program has the flexibility of the rehabilitation subsidy—either in terms of its depth or in permitting both modest and substantial rehabilitation.

Public Housing

Conventional public housing is similar in some ways to new housing built under the Section 8 Housing Assistance Program. In both programs, participation is conditioned by income, and the household is normally required to spend close to a quarter of its income on rent in exchange for living in a unit that meets program standards.

The construction and management of public housing are the responsibilities of a local housing authority, and the federal government provides a subsidy for 90 percent of the construction costs, plus some operating cost subsidy. Under Section 8, on the other hand, there is only a long-term lease arrangement by the local community with the owner of the new rental property, guaranteeing payment of rent *if* a participating household chooses a unit in the property.

The particular program designed here has new public housing units that are equivalent to about 5 percent of the base-year stock built over the simulated decade. Very low-income households are assumed to be the occupants of these additional units.[6] Because of low participant incomes and the high standards often embodied in public housing, improvement in the hous-

---

[6] Based on income figures for public housing tenants compiled for 1976 and deflated to 1970 (the terminal year of the simulation runs), it is estimated that about 40 percent of public housing tenants currently would be "very poor" (i.e., having 1976 total family incomes of $3,000 or less). For details on the 1976 income figures, see S. Loux and R. Sadacca, "Estimates of Rent and Tenant Income Levels in Public Housing Under Various Definitions" (Washington, D.C.: Urban Institute Working Paper 247-1, 1977).

ing situation of these tenants should be great.[7] The average subsidy payment will thus be large. One would expect additional public housing to have modest market effects because the households being removed from competition for privately owned dwellings initially are living in some of the least-desired units. Making these units available to other households is not likely to have much influence on their housing choices.

Many of the programs included here were designed to have approximately the same cost nationally. The only programs not included in this group are the major income maintenance program and Section 8 housing assistance. Note, however, that there can be considerable variation in the local (SMSA) cost of programs having the same aggregate national costs. Further, keeping the national costs roughly constant required juggling the exact terms of the subsidy. For example, to have the combined housing allowance-new construction program cost about the same as the exclusive housing allowance program, there had to be a less generous allowance program with fewer participants, to offset the cost of the capital subsidy for new units.

The most expensive program by far is the large-scale income maintenance program. Section 8, using the proportional allocation, has a national cost substantially less than that of the other programs reported here.

---

[7] It is often argued that the cost of public housing is higher than necessary because of the distortions in building techniques which subsidies for capital costs encourage. R. F. Muth in *Public Housing: An Economic Evaluation* (Washington, D.C.: The American Enterprise Institute, 1973) estimates public housing to be about 120 percent as expensive as it would be under a neutral type of subsidy. On the other hand, the U.S. General Accounting Office recently concluded the opposite in a long-term cost comparison of new Section 8 units and public housing. See *A Comparative Analysis of Subsidized Housing Costs* (Washington, D.C.: Program Analysis Division, General Accounting Office, 1976).

Finally, note that there has been considerable discussion about the value of increasing housing consumption through public housing. There have been several estimates of the relation between subsidy cost for public housing and the value public housing tenants place on the additional housing they receive. The estimates indicate that tenants could be equally well-off with a smaller cash subsidy than that embodied in the housing they receive; in other words, they value the housing subsidy at less than its resource cost. Two studies drawing this conclusion are: D. M. Barton and E. O. Olsen, "The Benefits and Costs of Public Housing in New York City" (Madison, Wis.: The Institute for Research on Poverty, University of Wisconsin, paper 372-76); and J. E. Adams, "The Performance of Public Housing in Small Cities: Net Tenant Benefits and Federal Expenditures," *Nebraska Journal of Economics and Business*, vol. 15, no. 3, pp. 59-71. Both of these analyses use the method developed by J. de Salvo in "A Methodology for Evaluating Housing Programs," *Journal of Regional Science* (1971), vol. 11, pp. 173-86.

Finally, note that all the simulations reported in this chapter are for the 1960-70 period. Each represents a program that is in operation over the 1960s (beyond those which actually did operate). In addition, each simulation shows how the presence of the program concerned would have altered the housing situation in a particular type of metropolitan area in 1970

COMPARING THE PROGRAMS

A qualitative comparison of the 10 programs in each of the two markets is presented in table 18. The focus is on a program's effects on lower-income households and on the amount of housing withdrawn from the stock as a result of that program.[8] Two groups of lower-income households are included. The first consists of program participants for each housing assistance program— e.g., housing allowances and Section 8. The second group, termed the "target population," includes roughly all households in the lowest income quartile. The entries for this group show the combined direct and indirect program effects for lower-income households. Both types of effects are important because some programs can provide major housing improvements to a few poor households, but only at the expense of worsening the situation for others.

In table 18 the average monthly subsidy payments to participating households indicate full costs only for demand-augmenting programs. For programs using a mix of consumer and supplier subsidies or supplier subsidies exclusively, the figures in entry D of the table (total program costs relative to the cost of a housing allowance) provide more comprehensive information.

There are five levels for the qualitative entries in the table, ranging from very high to very low. The table is organized so that, except for the two cost entries, a higher rating means that the program is "better." The extreme ratings—very high and very low—are used in only those few instances in which a program's effect is very different from that of any other program.

The overall qualitative classification of effects is based on comparing the particular effect (e.g., improvement in housing) of a given program to (1) the impact of other programs in that

---

[8] The number of additional model dwellings withdrawn is the same as the number of additional newly built units induced by the program.

Table 18
ALTERNATIVE POLICIES UNDER SHARPLY DIFFERENT MARKET CONDITIONS: COMPARISON OF EFFECTS[a]

City and Indicator	Housing Allowance	Income Maintenance		New Construction Subsidies				Rehabilitation Subsidy Combined with Housing Allowance	Section 8	Public Housing
		Small	Large	Across-the-Board	1-step Combined with Housing Allowance	1-step	2-step			
Textile City: High-Minority, Rapid-Growth										
A. Impact on participants[b]										
Average monthly subsidy	Moderate	Moderate	High	[e]	Low	[e]	[e]	Low	Moderate	Very High
Participation rate	High	High	High	[e]	High	[e]	[e]	High	High	High
Earmarking ratio[d]	Moderate	Moderate	Low	[e]	Moderate	[e]	[e]	Moderate	High	[e]
Improvement in housing consumption	Moderate	Low	Moderate	[e]	High	[e]	[e]	High	High	Very High
Control of price for housing services	High	High	High	[e]	High	[e]	[e]	High	High	[e]
B. Impact on target population[f]										
Improvement in housing consumption	High	Moderate	High	Moderate	High	Moderate	Low	High	Moderate	High
Control of price for housing services	High	High	High	High	High	High	High	High	High	[e]
C. Preservation of base-year housing stock[g]	Moderate	High	Moderate	Low	Moderate	Low	Low	High	Moderate	Moderate
D. Total program cost relative to cost of housing allowance[h]	—	Moderate	Very High	Low	Moderate	Moderate	Moderate	Moderate	Low	Moderate
Grain City: Low-Minority, Slow-Growth										

A. Impact on participants[b]									
Average monthly subsidy	Low	Low	High	Low	Low	Moderate	Low	Low	Very High
Participation rate[d]	High	High	High	High	High	Moderate	High	High	High
Earmarking ratio[d]	High	Low	Very Low	Low	Low	High	High	High	[e]
Improvement in housing consumption	Moderate	Low	Moderate	Moderate	Moderate	High	Low	High	Very High
Control of price for housing services	Low	Moderate	Low	Low	Low	Moderate	Low	Moderate	[e]
B. Impact on target population[f]									
Improvement in housing consumption	Moderate	Low	Moderate	Low	Moderate	Low	Very High	Moderate	High
Control of price for housing services	Low	Moderate	Low	High	High	Very High	Very High	Moderate	High
C. Preservation of base-year housing stock[g]	High	High	High	High	High	Moderate	Very High	Moderate	Moderate
D. Total program cost relative to cost of housing allowance[h]	—	High	Very High	High	High	Moderate	Moderate	Low	High

a Full description of programs simulated is provided in table 17. The simulations for Textile City assume that producers of housing from the existing stock are comparatively responsive to changes in demand; those in Steel City reflect the opposite assumption. All results are for the 1969-70 period.

b "Participants" are households participating in the program.

c Participants are not explicitly defined for this program.

d This is the ratio of the change in housing expenditures to subsidy received.

e Housing expenditures of participants generally decline under public housing. The earmarking ratio is not defined because the household is simply given a unit of a certain quantity of services; all of the subsidy produces more services. Because of the way in which public housing is valued, it is not possible to define a price per unit of housing services for public housing occupants.

f "Target population" is defined as the group eligible for participation under a national housing allowance program, with 22 percent of households eligible.

g This is equivalent to the number of newly built units induced by the program.

h This is the cost for a program in this type of housing market, *not* the cost of a national program. A "moderate" classification means the program costs about the same as the housing allowance program.

market on improving housing, and (2) general experience based
on a wide range of simulated programs in widely diverse
markets. Examples of the latter are a general knowledge of
participation rates and earmarking ratios[9] in entitlement programs. Obviously, a good deal of judgment is involved in the
classifications, and appendix F may be consulted for the numbers
on which the classifications are based.

It is extremely difficult to summarize briefly what the mass
of information in the table reveals about which programs should
be preferred in each market. At the risk of oversimplification, one
can begin by looking at which programs receive "high" ratings
on improving the housing situation of the target population—for
both increasing the quantity of services (consumption) and
controlling prices.

There are four such programs for the fast-growing, high-
minority city under an elastic supply assumption: housing
allowance, major income maintenance, housing allowance combined with a new construction subsidy, and housing allowance
combined with a rehabilitation subsidy. A fifth—the less costly
Section 8 program—nearly qualifies, and a larger Section 8 effort
(that referred to as the fair-share allocation in chapter 3)
certainly would. By contrast, only two programs help the target
population as much in the slow-growing, low-minority city under
an inelastic supply assumption: Section 8 and the combined
housing allowance-rehabilitation subsidy.[10]

Two points stand out from these assessments. One is that
the more successful programs are those involving actions which
both increase the demand for housing services and augment the
supply of dwellings where the increased demand is concentrated.
These are Section 8 and the housing allowance-supply subsidy
combinations. In this regard, it is important to note Section 8's
advantages of administrative simplicity and built-in coordination,
compared to the mixes of separate programs.

The second obvious point is that more programs work well
under rapidly growing, elastic supply situations than in the
opposite case. In particular, programs that only add to demand

---

[9] This is the ratio of increased housing expenditures to subsidy payments.

[10] Public housing has not been included in these lists because its effects
on consumption virtually are concentrated entirely on the two model households that were moved into public housing units. The resulting increases are
very large—enough to raise substantially the average housing level of the
target population. However, this average change is considered to be mis-
leading in terms of the actual situation of that population.

do well under these conditions, but not in the opposite situation.[11] The explanation for this difference has been noted earlier, but repetition may be useful. Cities with fast growing, moderate-to-low-income populations put a good deal of demand pressure on lower-quality housing. This pressure and the elastic supply of existing housing keeps the price per unit of service for low-quality units close to that for the rest of the market. Thus, introducing only programs that add to demand can cause a modest increase in the price of lower-quality housing before such shelter becomes competitive with the price per unit of service for new housing of the same size. Demand pressure causes construction of new housing, often for households with incomes only slightly above those of program participants. Because prices rise only modestly, the bulk of increased housing expenditures comes from improved housing quality.

On the other hand, cities with slow-growing, moderate- to low-income populations and inelastic supplies of existing housing often have a surplus of units in the lower-quality range. This surplus leads to a price per unit of service for lower-quality housing which is beneath that for housing in the rest of the market. Introducing a demand-stimulating program changes this situation. It causes prices at the bottom of the market to be driven up as the dwellings are improved. Since the prices were low to begin with, they have a longer distance to rise before new construction becomes a feasible alternative.

In some ways the price increase is desirable: Without it, landlords could not afford to improve their dwellings in order to meet program standards and the increased demands of participating households. Also, even with the increase, the price per unit of service for these dwellings is lower than in new units. Finally, the price rises keep older housing in the active stock. On the other hand, the price increases cause a substantial reduction in the share of increased housing expenditures going to increased quality.

The problem of achieving multiple objectives with individual housing programs is well illustrated by the impact on the housing supply of programs that get high marks for improving the housing situation of the target population. Only one program in both of the cities analyzed scores "high" on preserving the stock

---

[11] The one possible exception is an indication from the 1970-80 simulation of Section 8 that when prices are rising substantially in a rapid-growth market, the new construction sector may not respond adequately to subsidized demands from low-income households.

while also aiding the target population.[12] All the rest, however, score "moderate" on this criterion.

If the preservation objective were to be strongly emphasized, there are two programs (besides the one just noted) that get "high" marks on preservation and "moderate" marks on improving the housing of the target population. In Textile City (rapid growth), it is the small income maintenance program, and in Grain City (slow growth), it is the combined housing allowance and new construction subsidy. Of course, the weight one attaches to the preservation objective in practice would depend on the serviceable life of the lower-quality dwellings and the characteristics of the neighborhoods where they are located—factors that will vary sharply among metropolitan areas.

Another way of evaluating the effectiveness of programs that did not rate "high" in their aid to the target population is to ask how far below the "high" programs they actually are. In Textile City, using most of these less-effective programs—in particular, the small income maintenance program, the across-the-board capital subsidy, and the one-step capital subsidy—would not be too costly. All rate highly in controlling increases in the price per unit of housing service faced by the target population. They also rate "moderate" scores for increasing housing consumption.[13] On the other hand, a two-step capital subsidy produces only a small rise in the quantity of housing services consumed by the target population.[14]

In Grain City, one could do much worse if the wrong type of program is selected. All the programs designed to increase consumption by augmenting demand—housing allowances or the income maintenance programs—rate a "low" evaluation for either controlling prices or improving housing quality. Furthermore, all the programs relying exclusively on capital subsidies

---

[12] This is the combined rehabilitation and housing allowance program in the rapidly growing city.

[13] In practice, the "high" scores mean a 24-30 percent increase in the quantity of housing services consumed, while a "moderate" score means a 16-20 percent increase. ·

[14] The new construction subsidies can actually work to reduce consumption of the target population if these households are spending more than they wish on housing before introduction of the program. The rate at which the substitution occurs depends, in part, on how great this difference is, and in part, on how responsive housing consumption in general is to price changes. Under the two-step construction subsidy, the price reductions are particularly sharp, so that households are able to achieve the housing consumption level they want with no increase in expenditures, and generally with a decrease.

for new dwellings score "low" in increasing housing quality—i.e., the improvement never exceeds 5 percent. Put simply, these programs would be singularly inefficient in achieving their goals. The new construction subsidies, for example, would basically provide subsidies for new units that would have been built anyway. Any additional building would only serve to lower further the price per unit of housing services in the lower-quality portion of the market and would cause even more reductions in dwelling maintenance.

CONCLUSIONS

We draw three broad conclusions from the comparisons presented in this and earlier chapters. First, conditions in the individual metropolitan housing markets do indeed have a strong impact on the effectiveness of housing programs in (1) improving the housing situation of lower-income households and (2) preserving the housing stock.

Second, using a mix of actions to stimulate demand and supply (e.g., restricted or unrestricted cash transfers and actions that directly or indirectly make more suitable dwellings available to lower-income households) will generally be more effective than exclusive reliance on either demand- or supply-augmenting programs alone. This conclusion implies that there is considerable merit in the Section 8 Housing Assistance Program. In the event of a major welfare reform that increased housing demand, a strong case could be made for complementary, modest subsidies to suppliers to relieve market pressures, particularly in the slower-growing markets.[15]

Third, the best program appears to be one that allows local variation in the mix between (1) programs fueling housing demand and (2) those augmenting the supply of dwellings in the critical quality range. The argument for local determination certainly has merit, given local familiarity with immediate problems in the various housing markets. On this ground, the Section 8 program, with its locally prepared housing assistance plans, appears to be highly desirable.

---

[15] The argument here applies to *long-term* (10-year) effects, which should not be confused with short-run impacts. If a major increase in welfare were suddenly granted in a very tight housing market, the *short-term* response could easily be one of temporarily higher prices until new units could be built.

At the same time, it may be unrealistic now to believe that local planning officials have the resources to evaluate the long-term effects of strategies they put forward, or to make reasonably accurate projections of area shifts in household growth, income, and age distributions. These limitations argue persuasively for locally determined housing strategies that are within general guidelines set by (1) area trends in basic economic and demographic forces and (2) the potential long-term effects—both direct and indirect—of alternative strategies in similar metropolitan areas.

APPENDIX A
OVERVIEW OF THE MODEL

HOUSEHOLDS

Each model household represents several hundred or thousand actual households at the end of a decade. The exact number depends on the end-of-decade size of the metropolitan area to which the model is being applied, and the restriction that the model can efficiently handle a maximum of 40 to 45 households. A model household belongs to one of several household types; those used in applying the model to specific metropolitan areas include (1) white families under age 65, (2) white elderly and/or single-person households, (3) black families under age 65, and (4) black elderly and/or single-person households.[1]

Model households are further characterized by two *income measures*. One is an actual income figure: the actual mean end-of-period income for the households it represents, as reported in the U.S. Census. This figure is used to calculate the household's eligibility for certain government programs, the size of the subsidy it might receive, or income tax it might be required to pay. The second measure is a form of permanent or normal

---

[1] In the application to Austin, two additional types were defined for Chicano households.

household income, the measure relevant to the housing consumption of the household.[2]

The behavior of households in the model consists of deciding which of all possible dwellings to occupy. "All possible dwellings" includes a new dwelling of any desired level of services (subject to government-imposed minimum standards for new construction), as well as any of the existing dwellings in the model. The household makes its decision on the basis of the quantity of housing services that each dwelling offers, the price per unit at which those services are offered, the household's income, and three characteristics of the zone in which each dwelling is located.

The three important zone characteristics are (1) average travel time to and from work, (2) average net rent per dwelling, and (3) the proportion of zone residents belonging to the same racial group as the household making the choice. The first of these, travel time, is simply fed into the model as a piece of exogenous, or external, information about a zone. The other two characteristics are determined by the model itself, so that there is a two-way interaction between household choice and these zone characteristics. All the variables influencing household choices are combined into a utility function (one that *quantifies* the amount of enjoyment the household receives from each of these factors), which the household is attempting to maximize.

DWELLINGS

Each model dwelling, like each model household, represents several hundred or thousand actual cases—in fact, the number of actual cases per model unit is the same for dwellings as it is for households. Each model dwelling belongs to one of five or six zones that differ in accessibility, initial wealth of the occupants, and/or initial racial composition.

Each model is also characterized by the quantity of housing services it supplies at the beginning of the 10-year interval examined. The level of housing services of a dwelling, one of the basic concepts of the model, refers to an index of all the things of value that a physical structure provides—space, shelter,

---

[2] Actually, the measure used in the model is smoothed out more than necessary for the permanent-income concept. This additional smoothing is needed because of the elasticity of demand for housing implied by the particular form of the utility function used in the model. For details, see deLeeuw and Struyk, *The Web of Urban Housing.* (Also see later discussion of utility function in this appendix.)

privacy, design, and a host of others. The concept does not refer to the neighborhood characteristics associated with each dwelling; these are measured by the various attributes of the zone where a dwelling is located.

The behavior of the owners of existing dwellings is to make price-quantity offers with the goal of maximizing expected profits. Each price-quantity offer consists of (1) a quantity of housing services to be provided at the end of the decade to which the model refers and (2) a price at which that quantity will be provided. The offers thus resemble rental advertisements appearing in newspapers.

The price-quantity offers for each dwelling must lie along a supply schedule (i.e., a schedule of these price-quantity offers consistent with both housing-services technology and landlord expectations). The position of the schedule depends on (1) the initial quantity of housing services offered by the dwelling and (2) two parameters of the model, one representing the depreciation rate and the other related to the responsiveness of supply to a change in price.

The owner of each existing dwelling seeks to locate as high along the supply curve as possible—that is, to charge as high a price as possible without causing the dwelling to be vacant. Expected profits are an increasing function of this position along the supply curve. Competition among the owners of actual dwellings comprising each model dwelling is assumed sufficient to keep landlords from finding takers for offers above their supply curves and hence realizing excessive profits. Note that the model does not separate owner-occupants from renters; owner-occupants are in effect viewed as landlords renting to themselves.

The model includes a minimum price per unit of service, defined as just enough to cover the cost per unit of service to operate an existing dwelling. If dwelling owners cannot find occupants at any price at or above the minimum, their dwellings are withdrawn from the stock of housing. Withdrawal in actual housing markets can take the form of long-term vacancy, demolition, conversion to nonresidential use, or abandonment. The model does not distinguish among these different actions.

BUILDERS

The third actor in the model, the building industry, plays a more passive role than do model households and model dwellings.

The building industry is prepared to offer new dwellings at a fixed price per unit of service, so that the monthly total cost of a dwelling is proportional to the level of services provided. This treatment of the supply of new housing as being extremely responsive to demand over a 10-year period is consistent with available econometric evidence. The price per unit of service at which new dwellings are available is taken as a given for each housing market. Empirically, it is measured on the basis of HUD data on the cost per-square-foot of new dwellings.

This exogenous price per unit of housing service tends to set a ceiling for the price structure of the existing stock, although existing dwellings with especially favorable zone characteristics can command prices moderately above (usually 10 to 15 percent) the new construction price. New dwellings are assumed to be exclusively concentrated in a single "zone of new construction," which corresponds roughly to suburbanization.

GOVERNMENT

The model's final actor, government, can influence the housing location process at so many different points that it is impossible to describe its behavior succinctly. Tax charges, subsidy payments, transfer payments with or without earmarking them for housing, minimum new construction requirements, and minimum quantities of housing services in a particular zone are among the many ways government can affect housing markets in the model.

An income tax can be represented by replacing the actual income of a household with its income less the tax, before it enters the housing market. Tax rates and other aspects of tax formulas —for example, exemption levels—can be set separately for each household type, or even for each model household.

A transfer earmarked for housing—e.g., a housing allowance —can be represented by requiring an eligible household to consume at least some minimum level of housing services or spend some minimum amount on housing in order to receive the transfer. The household then determines its choices with and without the allowance and selects the most useful behavior.

Finally, a restrictive zoning ordinance can be represented by setting a minimum level of housing services for all dwellings in a zone. In brief, the model is exceptionally rich in the variety of government policies it can handle.

SOLUTION PROCESS

A solution of the model, as mentioned earlier, is a situation in which none of the four actors has any incentive to change position. Each household is the unique occupant of one dwelling, the one which maximizes its satisfaction, given all the price-quantity offers facing it. The owner of each existing dwelling is charging the highest price possible (i.e., as high along the supply curve as possible) without finding the dwelling vacant (if it is vacant even at the lowest point on its supply schedule, the unit is withdrawn from the stock). The building industry is supplying the number of new dwellings that households are willing to purchase. Government regulations are being strictly enforced.

The computer program to solve the model searches for a solution with these properties, through a process of trial and error. Departures from solution conditions in one trial govern the way the solution is modified for the next trial. The steps in the search process have no theoretical or empirical significance; a housing market may search for a solution in a different way than does the computer program. Only the final solution of a problem is of interest. Once the program finds a solution, the results can be tabulated in a variety of ways, depending on their use: prices, quantities, and locations can be shown by household, by dwelling, by zone, by household type, or, in the case of certain subsidy programs, by household eligibility and participation status.

APPENDIX B
CLASSIFICATION OF U.S. SMSAS INTO FOUR PROTOTYPE CITIES

In this appendix, all 1970 SMSAs are placed into four categories based on (1) the proportion of nonwhite population and (2) the growth rate of low- to moderate-income households over the 1960s. A population-weighted sample of SMSAs was used to estimate the average nonwhite percentage (12 percent) and the average growth of households with real incomes below $10,000 (in 1970 dollars) during the 1960s (4 percent). All SMSAs were then classified high- or low-minority, on the basis of whether their nonwhite proportions were greater or less than 12 percent. They were also classified as rapid- or slow-growth, depending on whether their population with real 1970 incomes of $10,000 or less grew by more or less than 4 percent.

The data source on the percentage of an SMSA population that is not white is U.S. Bureau of the Census, *County and City Data Book, 1972*, U.S. Government Printing Office, Washington, D.C., 1973, table 3.

The data sources on the growth of households with real incomes below $10,000 (1970 dollars) during the 1960s are table 3 of the *County and City Data Book, 1972*; the Census Bureau's 1960 census, volume I, *Characteristics of the Population*, part 1, United States Summary, table 148; and additionally for SMSAs with boundary changes, parts 2-52 (state books), table 86. The

1970 SMSA boundaries were applied to 1960. The 1960 real income equivalent of $10,000 in 1970, as used in the calculations, is $7,000.

These sources give incomes for families, not households. The number of families with incomes below $7,000 in 1960 and $10,000 in 1970 was used to calculate a percentage change in families with real incomes below $10,000 (1970 dollars). This was adjusted to households by using the difference for all SMSAs between the growth in households and families. The amount of 12 percentage points (4.3 percent growth for households and 7.7 percent decline for families) was added to the growth rate of families in each SMSA to estimate that area's growth of low- to moderate-income households. Sources for the growth rate of U.S. households are U.S. Bureau of the Census, *U.S. Census of Housing: 1960*, vol. II, *Metropolitan Housing*, part 1, United States and Divisions, table A-7 and the corresponding 1970 report, table A-6.

HIGH-MINORITY, RAPID-GROWTH

Albany, Ga. (35, 12)*
Atlanta, Ga. (22, 12)
Augusta, Ga.-S.C. (28, 11)
Baton Rouge, La. (29, 19)
Biloxi-Gulfport, Miss. (17, 14)
Bryan-College Station, Tex.
    (17, 24)
Charleston, S.C. (32, 12)
Charlotte, N.C. (23, 13)
Chattanooga, Tenn. (16, 5)
Cleveland, Ohio (16, 15)
Columbia, S.C. (26, 18)
Columbus, Ga.-Ala. (29, 8)
Columbus, Ohio (12, 9)
Dallas, Tex. (17, 11)
Durham, N.C. (28, 44)
Fayetteville, N.C. (26, 35)
Fort Lauderdale-Hollywood,
    Fla. (13, 42)

Gainesville, Fla. (21, 27)
Galveston-Texas City, Tex.
    (20, 7)
Greenville, S.C. (15, 5)
Honolulu, Hawaii (58, 12)
Houston, Tex. (20, 37)
Huntsville, Ala. (16, 21)
Jackson, Miss. (37, 12)
Jacksonville, Fla. (23, 14)
Kansas City, Mo.-Kans. (13, 6)
Lafayette, La. (23, 22)
Lawton, Okla. (14, 35)
Lexington, Ky. (13, 17)
Little Rock-N. Little Rock, Ark.
    (19, 16)
Macon, Ga. (29, 11)
Memphis, Tenn.-Ark. (38, 16)
Miami, Fla. (15, 19)
Mobile, Ala. (30, 10)

---

* The first number in parentheses is the proportion of nonwhites in 1970; the second is the estimated percentage change (increase or decrease) during the 1960s in the number of low- to moderate-income households.

HIGH-MINORITY, RAPID-GROWTH (continued)

Monroe, La. (27, 12)
Orlando, Fla. (15, 22)
Pensacola, Fla. (18, 24)
Petersburg, Colonial Heights,
  Va. (32, 17)
Pine Bluff, Ark. (41, 7)
Raleigh, N.C. (22, 15)
Richmond, Va. (25, 10)
San Francisco-Oakland, Calif.
  (17, 5)
Shreveport, La. (33, 7)

Tallahassee, Fla. (26, 36)
Tuscaloosa, Ala. (24, 7)
Tyler, Tex. (24, 8)
Vineland-Milleville, Brighton,
  N.J. (15, 4)
Washington, D.C.-Md.-Va.
  (26, 13)
West Palm Beach, Fla. (18, 30)
Wilmington, Del.-N.J.-Md.
  (13, 26)
Wilmington, N.C. (24, 11)

LOW-MINORITY, SLOW-GROWTH

Abilene, Tex. (6, 2) *
Akron, Ohio (8, —9)
Albany-Schenectady-Troy,
  N.Y. (4, —8)
Allentown-Bethlehem-Easton,
  Pa.-N.J. (1, —6)
Altoona, Pa. (1, —14)
Anderson, Ind. (6, 3)
Appleton-Oshkosh, Wis.
  (1, —1)
Bay City, Mich. (1, —7)
Binghamton, N.Y. (1, —4)
Boston, Mass. (5, —11)
Bridgeport, Conn. (8, —8)
Bristol, Conn. (1, —14)
Brockton, Mass. (2, —5)
Buffalo, N.Y. (9, —5)
Canton, Ohio (6, —2)
Cedar Rapids, Iowa (1, —3)
Charleston, W. Va. (6, 3)
Cincinnati, Ohio-Ky.-Ind.
  (11, —2)
Danbury, Conn. (4, —12)

Davenport-Rock Island-Moline,
  Iowa.-Ill. (4, 1)
Dayton, Ohio (12, 0)
Decatur, Ill. (8, —10)
Des Moines, Iowa (4, —5)
Dubuque, Iowa (0, —4)
Erie, Pa. (4, 3)
Evansville, Ind.-Ky. (6, 2)
Fall River, Mass.-R.I. (1, —4)
Fargo-Morehead, N. Dak.-
  Minn. (1, 2)
Fort Wayne, Ind. (7, 1)
Grand Rapids, Mich. (5, —3)
Green Bay, Wis. (1, 2)
Harrisburg, Pa. (7, —3)
Hartford, Conn. (8, 2)
Jackson, Mich. (6, —4)
Jersey City, N.J. (11, —5)
Johnstown, Pa. (1, 12)
Kalamazoo, Mich. (5, 0)
LaCrosse, Wis. (1, 3)
Lancaster, Pa. (2, 2)
Lansing, Mich. (4, —4)

---

* The first number in parentheses is the proportion of nonwhites in
1970; the second is the estimated percentage change (increase or decrease)
during the 1960s in the number of low- to moderate-income households.

LOW-MINORITY, SLOW-GROWTH (continued)

Lawrence-Haverhill, Mass.-
N.H. (1, —4)
Lewiston-Auburn, Maine (0, 1)
Lima, Ohio (6, —9)
Lincoln, Nebr. (2, —6)
Lorain-Elyria, Ohio (7, —4)
Manchester, N.H. (0, —3)
Meriden, Conn. (3, —12)
Milwaukee, Wis. (8, —4)
Minneapolis-St. Paul, Minn.
(3, —3)
Muskegon-Muskegon Heights,
Mich. (11, —1)
Nashua, N.H. (0, —4)
New Bedford, Mass. (3, —5)
New Britain, Conn. (3, —6)
Norwalk, Conn. (9, —7)
Paterson-Clifton-Passaic, N.J.
(6, —5)
Peoria, Ill. (5, —8)
Pittsburgh, Pa. (7, —5)
Pittsfield, Mass. (2, —8)
Portland, Maine (0, —28)
Racine, Wis. (7, 2)
Reading, Pa. (2, —9)
Rochester, Minn. (1, 0)
Rochester, N.Y. (7, —6)
Rockford, Ill. (6, 1)
St. Joseph, Mo. (3, —5)

Scranton, Pa. (1, —6)
Sherman-Denison, Tex. (8, 4)
Sioux City, Iowa-Nebr. (2, —9)
Sioux Falls, S. Dak. (1, 1)
South Bend, Ind. (7, —2)
Spokane, Wash. (2, 2)
Springfield, Ill. (5, —7)
Springfield, Mo. (2, 0)
Springfield, Ohio (9, 3)
Springfield-Chicopee-Holyoke,
Mass.-Conn. (5, —3)
Stamford, Conn. (8, —5)
Steubenville-Weirton, Ohio-
W. Va. (4, 1)
Syracuse, N.Y. (4, 1)
Terre Haute, Ind. (3, —8)
Toledo, Ohio-Mich. (9, —6)
Topeka, Kans. (8, 3)
Utica-Rome, N.Y. (3, 3)
Waterloo, Iowa (5, 1)
Wheeling, W. Va.-Ohio (2, —6)
Wichita Falls, Tex. (8, 4)
Wilkes Barre-Hazleton, Pa.
(1, —7)
Worcester, Mass. (1, —14)
Youngstown-Warren, Ohio
(10, —6)
York, Pa. (3, —11)

HIGH-MINORITY, SLOW-GROWTH

Atlantic City, N.J. (18, 2) *
Baltimore, Md. (24, 0)
Beaumont-Port Arthur-
Orange, Tex. (22, 4)

Birmingham, Ala. (30, 2)
Chicago, Ill. (18, —1)
Detroit, Mich. (19, —12)
Flint, Mich. (13, —5)

---

* The first number in parentheses is the proportion of nonwhites in 1970; the second is the estimated percentage change (increase or decrease) during the 1960s in the number of low- to moderate-income households.

HIGH-MINORITY SLOW-GROWTH (continued)

Gadsden, Ala. (14, 0)
Gary-Hammond-E. Chicago,
   Ill. (18, —6)
Greensboro, N.C. (20, 4)
Indianapolis, Ind. (12, 3)
Lake Charles, La. (22, 1)
Los Angeles-Long Beach, Calif.
   (14, 3)
Louisville, Ky.-Ind. (12, 3)
Lynchburg, Va. (20, 4)
Montgomery, Ala. (35, —7)
Nashville-Davidson, Tenn.
   (18, —6)
New Haven, Conn. (12, —2)

New York, N.Y. (18, —2)
Newark, N.J. (19, —3)
Newport News-Hampton, Va.
   (26, —27)
Norfolk-Portsmouth, Va.
   (26, —2)
Philadelphia, Pa. (18, —2)
Saginaw, Mich. (12, —15)
St. Louis, Mo. (16, —3)
Savannah, Ga. (35, 2)
Texarkana, Tex.-Ark. (22, 2)
Trenton, N.J. (17, 1)
Waco, Tex. (16, —1)

LOW-MINORITY, RAPID-GROWTH

Albuquerque, N. Mex. (4, 22)*
Amarillo, Tex. (5, 7)
Anaheim-Santa Ana-Garden
   Grove, Calif. (3, 50)
Ann Arbor, Mich. (9, 6)
Asheville, N.C. (9, 14)
Austin, Tex. (11, 21)
Bakersfield, Calif. (7, 17)
Billings, Mont. (2, 17)
Bloomington-Normal, Ill.
   (2, 17)
Boise City, Idaho (1, 10)
Brownsville-Harlingen-San
   Benito, Tex. (1, 5)
Champaign-Urbana, Ill. (8, 28)
Colorado Springs, Col. (6, 33)
Columbia, Mo. (6, 11)
Corpus Christi, Tex. (5, 10)
Denver, Col. (5, 5)

Duluth-Superior, Minn.-Wis.
   (1, 18)
El Paso, Tex. (4, 22)
Eugene, Oreg. (2, 24)
Fitchburg-Leominster, Mass.
   (1, 11)
Fort Smith, Ark.-Okla. (7, 4)
Fort Worth, Tex. (11, 10)
Fresno, Calif. (8, 14)
Great Falls, Mont. (3, 14)
Hamilton-Middleton, Ohio
   (5, 7)
Huntington-Ashland, W. Va.-
   Ky.-Ohio (3, 40)
Kenosha, Wis. (2, 17)
Knoxville, Tenn. (7, 11)
Lafayette-W. Lafayette, Ind.
   (2, 9)
Laredo, Tex. (1, 21)

* The first number in parentheses is the proportion of nonwhites in 1970; the second is the estimated percentage change (increase or decrease) during the 1960s in the number of low- to moderate-income households.

LOW-MINORITY, RAPID-GROWTH (continued)

Las Vegas, Nev. (10, 21)
Lowell, Mass. (1, 13)
Lubbock, Tex. (8, 16)
Madison, Wis. (2, 5)
Mansfield, Ohio (7, 5)
McAllen-Pharr-Edinburg, Tex. (0, 10)
Midland, Tex. (10, 5)
Modesto, Calif. (2, 16)
Muncie, Nev. (6, 4)
New London-Groton-Norwich, Conn. (4, 40)
Odessa, Tex. (5, 5)
Ogden, Utah (3, 9)
Oklahoma City, Okla. (11, 15)
Omaha, Neb.-Iowa (8, 5)
Owensboro, Ky. (4, 6)
Oxnard-Ventura, Calif. (4, 43)
Phoenix, Ariz. (5, 35)
Portland, Oreg.-Wash. (4, 9)
Providence-Pawtucket-Warwick, R.I. Mass. (3, 14)
Provo-Orem, Utah (1, 25)
Pueblo, Col. (2, 7)
Reno, Nev. (4, 38)

Roanoke, Va. (12, 24)
Sacramento, Calif. (9, 32)
Salem, Oreg. (1, 33)
Salinas-Monterey, Calif. (10, 19)
Salt Lake City, Utah (2, 16)
San Angelo, Tex. (5, 12)
San Antonio, Tex. (8, 19)
San Bernardino, Riverside, Ontario, Calif. (6, 23)
San Diego, Calif. (7, 26)
San Jose, Calif. (6, 24)
Santa Barbara, Calif. (4, 37)
Santa Rosa, Calif. (3, 22)
Seattle-Everett, Wash. (6, 7)
Stockton, Calif. (11, 13)
Tacoma, Wash. (7, 13)
Tampa-St. Petersburg, Fla. (11, 21)
Tucson, Ariz. (6, 23)
Tulsa, Okla. (11, 10)
Vallejo-Napa, Calif. (11, 17)
Waterbury, Conn. (6, 27)
Wichita, Kans. (8, 15)

APPENDIX C
PROJECTION OF KEY MODEL INPUT USED IN CHAPTER 5

HOUSEHOLD INCOME DISTRIBUTION

Another model, DYNASIM, was used to make projections of household incomes. DYNASIM is designed to depict particular elements of the status of persons and families and their economic and demographic behavioral characteristics. Using macroeconomic forecasts as inputs, DYNASIM can, in effect, "grow" families into the future, tracing their eventual demographic and economic changes by applying previously estimated behavioral relationships to each household on a probabilistic basis.[1] The projections of household incomes as of 1980 were a byproduct of an analysis of future ADC case loads; only minor additional tabulations with the file of 1980 households were needed to obtain income distributions for each of the four household types used in the model.[2]

---

[1] A general description of this model is in H. Guthrie, "Microanalysis Simulation Modeling for Evaluation of Public Policy," *Urban Affairs Quarterly* (June 1972), pp. 403-17. A full description is in G. Orcutt, S. Caldwell, R. F. Wertheimer, II, et al., *Policy Exploration Through Microanalytic Simulation* (Washington, D.C.: The Urban Institute, 1976).

[2] For details see R. F. Wertheimer, II and S. R. Zedlewski, "The Impact of Demographic Change on the Distribution of Earned Income and the AFDC Program: 1975-1985" (Washington, D.C.: Urban Institute Working Paper 985-1, 1976).

The top part of table C-1 shows the level and percentage change in the mean real and money incomes of households over the 1960s, calculated from decennial census and current population survey (CPS) data. The same level and percentage change over the 1970s comes from the DYNASIM forecast, deflated to 1979.[3] Rather surprisingly, these data show the real income growth in the present decade to be roughly the same as that during the 1960s. This is surprising because there was virtually no growth in real income between 1969 and 1974, as shown in table C-2. Further, the 1970-74 period was apparently less favorable for real income growth than was 1960-64, as suggested by the plot of median incomes since 1951 in figure C-1. Finally, there is little expectation that income growth over 1975-79 period will approach that of the late 1960s.

To check the plausibility of the DYNASIM forecast, the growth in average household income for the 1960-70 and 1970-80 periods was computed, using personal income data from national income accounts and figures on the total number of households from the decennial census and census projections.[4] The results of these calculations, shown in the lower part of table C-1, are more consistent with expectations, showing a 17 percent growth in real income during the 1970s, compared with a 26.5 percent rise over the 1960s.

The macro forecast used by DYNASIM and that employed in the computations just described are essentially identical, so the difference in income growth rates lies elsewhere. These three features of the DYNASIM calculations might account for the discrepancy:

1. The model uses somewhat different definitions of families and primary individuals than the standard definitions used by the Census Bureau;

2. DYNASIM necessarily makes assumptions about the participation and benefit levels of a host of welfare and income-transfer programs, and those assumptions might turn out to be too high; and

---

[3] Deflation was effected by the change in the consumer price index, plus an additional 2 percent adjustment for increased real income—roughly equivalent to the projected rise in productivity in 1980.

[4] Use of the decennial census household data dictated using the years 1960 and 1970 instead of 1959 and 1969. From figure C-1, it is fairly clear that this change should have very modest effects on the 10-year percentage change calculations.

Table C-1

CALCULATED CHANGES IN AVERAGE HOUSEHOLD
INCOME, 1960-70 AND 1970-80

Change	Current Dollars	1967 Dollars[a]
Micro Household Data		
Income levels		
1959 census[b]	6,200	6,989
1969		
CPS[c]	9,759	8,391
Census[d]	10,136	8,751
1979—DYNASIM	21,260	10,721
Percentage change		
1959-69[e]		
CPS	57.4	20.0
Census	63.4	24.6
1969-79[f]		
CPS	117.8	27.7
Census	109.7	22.5
National accounts personal income and aggregate household counts data[g]		
Income levels		
1960-GNP data[h]	7,446	8,394
1970-GNP data[h]	12,354	10,622
1980-DRI estimate[i]	24,645	12,432
Percentage change		
1960-70	65.9	26.5
1970-80	99.5	17.0

[a]These dollars are deflated, using Consumer Price Index.
[b]See U.S. Bureau of the Census, U.S. Census of Housing: 1960, vol. II, *Metropolitan Housing*, part 1, table A-3 (Washington, D.C.: U.S. Government Printing Office, 1963).
[c]See U.S. Bureau of the Census, *Current Population Reports*, P-60 Series, no. 101, tables 24 and 32, "Money Income in 1974 of Families and Persons in the United States" (Washington, D.C.: U.S. Government Printing Office, 1976).
[d]See U.S. Bureau of the Census, U.S. Census of Housing: 1970, *Metropolitan Housing Characteristics*, HC(2)-1, (Washington, D.C.: U.S. Government Printing Office, 1973).
[e]1959 census data are used in both computations.
[f]1979 DYNASIM data are used in both computations.
[g]Number of households for 1960 and 1970 is from decennial Census reports cited in notes b and d; for 1980, see U.S. Bureau of the Census, *Current Population Reports*, P-25 Series, no. 607, "Projections of the Number of Households and Families: 1975 to 1990" (Washington, D.C.: U.S. Government Printing Office, 1975).
[h]See *Economic Report of the President*, table B-15 (Washington, D.C.: U.S. Government Printing Office, 1976).
[i]See Data Resources, Inc., forecast of May 1976.

Figure C-1

MEDIAN FAMILY INCOMES, 1951–74

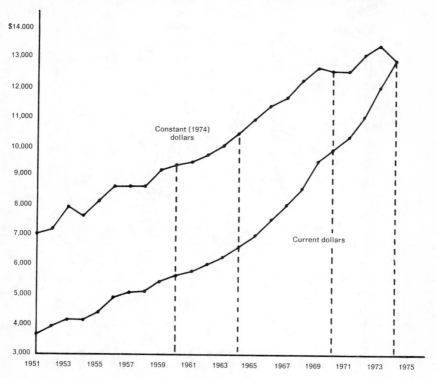

Source: U.S. Bureau of the Census, *Current Population Reports*, P-60
Series, no. 101, tables 24 and 32," Money Incomes in 1974 of Fam-
ilies and Persons in the United States" (Washington, D.C.: U.S.
Government Printing Office, 1976).

Table C-2

PERCENTAGE CHANGE IN INCOME, 1969-74, BY HOUSEHOLD TYPE

| | Number of households (in thousands) | | Mean income | | | | Percentage change, 1969-74 | |
| | | | Money | | Real[a] | | Money income | Real income |
	1969	1974	1969	1974	1969	1974		
Whites								
Families								
Total	46,022	49,451	10,953	15,047	10,021	9,334	37.3	−6.8
Over age 65	6,515	7,319	6,927	9,998	6,338	6,202	44.3	−2.1
Under age 65	39,507	42,312	11,616	15,924	10,628	9,878	37.0	−7.0
Primary individuals,								
Total	10,319	13,611	4,562	6,436	4,174	3,992	41.0	−4.3
Elderly families plus								
primary individuals	16,834	20,930	5,477	7,681	5,011	4,764	40.2	−4.9
Blacks								
Families								
Total	4,774	5,498	6,971	9,515	6,378	5,902	36.4	−7.4
Over age 65	507	641	4,205	6,601	3,846	4,095	56.9	6.4
Under age 65	4,267	4,857	7,300	9,899	6,679	6,141	35.6	−8.0
Primary individuals,								
Total	1,309	1,793	3,044	4,628	2,785	2,871	52.0	3.0
Elderly families plus								
primary individuals	1,816	2,434	3,368	5,148	3,081	3,193	52.8	3.6

Source: U.S. Bureau of the Census, *Current Population Reports*, P-60 Series, nos. 75 and 101, "Income in 1969 of Families and Persons in the United States," and, "Money Income in 1974 of Families and Persons in the United States" (Washington, D.C.: U.S. Government Printing Office, 1970 and 1976).

[a] Deflated with the consumer price index, 1967=100.

3. The model uses fairly short-term experience with wealth accumulation as the basis for its wealth predictions to 1980.[5]

The requisite information or resources are not available to determine the actual cause of the difference in income growth rates. Thus, a procedure has been adopted that uses the average real income increase indicated by personal income data and the DYNASIM income distribution, appropriately deflated for consistency with the average growth rate.

Finally, table C-3 lists the model households used in these analyses by their 1980 incomes for the two prototype cities used.

Table C-3

ANNUAL HOUSEHOLD INCOME BY CITY, HOUSEHOLD TYPE, AND YEAR

White nonelderly			White elderly and single		Nonwhite nonelderly		Nonwhite elderly and single
Textile City: 1980, high-minority, rapid-growth							
$ 2,888	19,426	35,401	$ 1,696	12,298	$ 2,600	17,336	$ 2,657
4,964	21,594	37,338	3,344	15,606	4,841	22,735	16,086
7,058	25,937	39,272	4,378	20,133	7,267	31,853	
8,978	25,724	41,208	5,658	25,620	9,583	42,591	
10,967	27,659	43,143	7,564	34,427	12,864		
13,007	29,594	45,078	9,614	43,446			
15,090	31,530	47,014					
17,256	33,466						
Steel City: 1980, high-minority, slow-growth							
$ 3,205	19,004	34,379	$ 2,010	15,013	$ 2,953		$ 2,657
5,816	21,774	36,583	3,880	20,897	5,849		16,085
8,398	24,473	39,326	5,417	29,917	8,883		
10,910	26,960	41,799	7,891	41,943	12,889		
13,519	29,433	44,272	10,908		18,837		
16,232	31,906	46,745			27,497		
					41,057		

DISTRIBUTION OF HOUSEHOLD TYPES

The model generally distinguishes four household types on the basis of differences among them in ratios of housing expenditures to income. The four types are (1) white nonelderly house-

---

[5] To examine the effect of these assumptions, the 1974 income distributions predicted by DYNASIM, which began with a 1970 population, were contrasted with those reported in the *Current Population Reports*. This comparison was limited by the large size of some of the income intervals required for interval matching, but the general picture that emerged was one of general comparability. It is possible that the 1980 projections are more heavily influenced by the fact that DYNASIM assumptions differ further from those of the macroestimate.

holds, (2) white elderly and single-person households, (3) black
nonelderly households, and (4) black elderly and single-person
households. The projections to be made must modify the 1970
household distribution in each of the four prototype cities. The
strategy is to apply the national rate of shift among household
types to the base-year distribution in each of the four cities.

The census has projected the distribution of households among
more household types than are used in the model, but no distinction is made by race.[6] To effect the race separation required a
procedure of several steps. First, using decennial census data for
1960 and CPS data for 1975, we computed for each of the two
years the distribution of households among the four household
types used in the model.[7] The average annual change in the proportion of households in each type over the 1960-75 period was
assumed to hold between 1976 and 1980, and the rates of change
were applied to the 1975 distribution of households by type, to
obtain the 1980 distribution.

To compare these estimates with the census projections, we
combined projections of black and white households into nonelderly household and elderly/single-person household categories,
using as weights the projected proportions of blacks and whites
as of 1980. Part B of table C-4 shows the two sets of projections
to be in close accord. The trend to 1980 in the division of black
and white households between nonelderly families and elderly/
singles will continue to be away from nonelderly families, as it
has since 1960.

The change in the mix of households by race was projected
by using the 1960-70 change in the ratio of black to total households as a base, and adjusting that change downward slightly
for the reduced rate of black migration, as recently documented.[8]
Thus the proportion of all black households in our two high-

[6] U.S. Bureau of the Census, *Current Population Reports*, P-25 Series,
no. 67, table 2, series B, "Projections of the Number of Households and
Families: 1975-1990" (Washington, D.C.: U.S. Government Printing Office,
1975).

[7] U.S. Bureau of the Census, 1960 Census of Housing, *Metropolitan
Housing Characteristics*, HC(2)-1, United States and Regions (Washington,
D.C.: U.S. Government Printing Office, 1962); U.S. Bureau of the Census,
Current Population Reports, P-20 Series, no. 287, table 2, "Marital Status
and Living Arrangements: March 1975" (Washington, D.C.: U.S. Govern-
ment Printing Office, 1975).

[8] Social and Economic Statistics Administration, U.S. Bureau of the
Census, *The Social and Economic Status of the Black Population in the U.S.,
1971 and 1974*, P-23 Series, nos. 42 and 54 (Washington, D.C.: U.S. Government Printing Office, 1972 and 1974).

Table C-4
HOUSEHOLD DISTRIBUTION BY TYPE, 1960-80

A. Distribution of Households Nationally Over Time

	Blacks			Whites		
	1960[a]	1970[a]	1980[b]	1960[a]	1970[a]	1980[b]
Families, head						
Under age 65	.747	.707	.650	.746	.707	.642
Age 65 and older	.102	.101	.082	.121	.118	.114
Primary individuals						
Under age 65	.110	.129	.193	.075	.094	.142
Age 65 and older	.041	.062	.074	.056	.080	.101
Total	1.00	1.00	1.00	1.00	1.00	1.00

B. Comparison of Projections for 1980

	Projection	
	Racially disaggregated[b]	Census[c]
Families, head		
Under age 65	.64	.66
Age 65 and older	.11	.11
Primary individuals		
Under age 65	.15	.14
Age 65 and older	.10	.09

[a]Data are from the U.S. Bureau of the Census, U.S. Census of Housing: 1970, *Metropolitan Housing Characteristics*, HC(2)-1, "United States and Regions" (Washington, D.C.: U.S. Government Printing Office, 1962 and 1972).
[b]Projection described in text is based on separate data for black and whites.
[c]Data are from the U.S. Bureau of the Census, *Current Population Reports*, P-25 Series, no. 607, "Projections of the Number of Households and Families: 1975 to 1990" (Washington, D.C.: U.S. Government Printing Office, 1975).

minority prototype cities shifts from 14 percent in 1960 to 20 percent in 1970 to 25 percent in 1980. The 1980 model households are shown in the section describing the estimate of the 1980 income distribution (table C-3).

PROJECTING GROWTH IN NUMBER OF HOUSEHOLDS

These projections were the least complicated of those made, since the Bureau of Economic Analysis (BEA) has projected the 1980 population of most of the metropolitan areas in the country.[9]

[9] Bureau of Economic Analysis, U.S. Department of Commerce, *Area Economic Projections to 1990* (Washington, D.C.: U.S. Government Printing Office, 1975).

Given the availability of these figures, the strategy was to compute the ratio of the percentage change in households (1960-70) to the percentage change in population for the same period (based on decennial census data), and then to multiply this ratio by the 1970-80 percentage change in population, calculated with the BEA data. These computations were made for each of the SMSAs on which the four hypothetical cities were based, and the average was then taken for each subset of SMSAs representing one prototype city. Note that the projections are for the cohorts of SMSAs with growth rates above and below the median rates in the 1960s, not for comparable cities during the 1970s.

The numerical values of these computations are shown in entries 2-6 in table C-5 for the two hypothetical cities used in the text analysis. Over the 1970s, a 13 percent increase in the number of households in the rapidly growing city and an 8 percent increase in the slow-growing city is forecast (entry 6). This represents a sharp decline in household growth in both cities compared with that in the 1960s, when these values were 27 and 13 percent, respectively.

There is, however, one complication in using these projected

Table C-5
GROWTH IN NUMBER OF HOUSEHOLDS, 1970-80

	High-minority cities	
	Rapid-growth	Slow-growth
1. Percentage change in model households used in simulations, 1960-70	25	7
2. Actual percentage change in households, 1960-70	27	13
3. Percentage change in population, 1960-70	23	11
4. Ratio: 2/3	1.17	1.18
5. Percentage change in population, 1970-80	11	6
6. Percentage change in households, 1970-80 (4 × 5)	13	7
7. Model households in 1980		
a. Total	46	36
b. Distribution by household type		
white nonelderly families	23	18
white elderly families/ single individuals	12	9
black nonelderly families	9	7
black elderly families/ single individuals	2	2

growth rates to contrast the experience of these two prototype cities during the 1960s and 1970s. Comparing the household growth rates used in the simulations done for the 1960s (entry 1) with the actual growth rates (entry 2) shows that the first value is only half the actual value for the slow-growing city. The problem causing the discrepancy arose in the initial procedure of constructing the slow-growing city. The procedure focused on matching the growth in low- to moderate-income households in the actual cities with the model households in the hypothetical cities. (It seems that simulation results proved to be more sensitive to variations in the number of households in this income range than to shifts in the total number of households.) [10]

In achieving this objective, the secondary goal of matching overall growth rates was not attained. For this reason, the comparison for the 1960-70 and 1970-80 experience for the slow-growing city is somewhat imprecise. We stress, however, that the housing situation of the lower-income households—the group with which we are most concerned—would be quite insensitive to the addition of several model households with higher incomes. Such an addition would probably result principally in the construction of an equal number of new dwellings over the period.

FACTOR INPUT PRICES

The model requires exogenous information on the average price per unit of service for capital (P_c) and operating (P_o) inputs to new housing built over the decade. In past applications of the model, these data have been derived from the capital and operating costs of units insured under FHA's Section 203(b) program,[11] the unsubsidized program for owner-occupied homes in one-to-four-unit structures. Note that a technique has been developed for converting the average dwellings insured in a given year into a "standard" dwelling, so that a price index results.[12]

In the present work, FHA data are again used, adjusted as in the past. For comparative purposes, data from the Bureau of

---

[10] For a full description of the construction of the hypothetical cities, see deLeeuw and Struyk, *The Web of Urban Housing*, a summary of which is given in chapter 2 of this study.

[11] FHA is the Federal Housing Administration, part of HUD.

[12] See R. Struyk, "A Comparison of FHA and BLS Price Indices of Owner Occupied Housing in Urban Areas" (Washington, D.C.: Urban Institute Working Paper 208-7, 1972).

Labor Statistics (BLS) for the owner-occupant component of the Consumer Price Index (CPI) are also used. One important difference in the two series is that the BLS includes recently purchased new and existing units in its sample, while the comparable FHA sample includes new units only. In addition, there is probably much variation in the quality of units in each sample, despite adjustment of the FHA and BLS sampling procedures. For these reasons the two have not moved in lock-step over the period for which we have data, as shown in figure C-2.[13]

The general procedure followed in projecting the prices has been to estimate the relationship between P_c or P_o and real gross national product (GNP), the CPI, or the GNP deflator for the 1959-73 period, using regression analysis. The values for P_c and P_o were then calculated for the 1974-79 period by taking the values of the independent variables projected by macroeconomic models of the entire economy and substituting those values in the regression models.

Table C-6 shows the regression models actually selected. The only independent variable is the CPI. Other models that included additional variables were plagued by high correlations among

Table C-6

REGRESSION ANALYSIS OF RELATION BETWEEN MOVEMENT IN FACTOR INPUT PRICES AND CONSUMER PRICE INDEX

	Operating inputs		Capital inputs	
	FHA	BLS	FHA	BLS
Constant	−41.3	−21.4	−94.9	8.41
	(7.57)	(6.53)	(6.47)	(.98)
CPI	.97	1.22	1.86	.93
	(19.8)	(39.4)	(13.4)	(11.1)
R^2	.97	.99	.94	.92
F-statistic	390	1152	198	123
Durbin-Watson	2.77	.84	.96	.85
Degrees of Freedom	11	11	11	11

[13] The FHA data are from HUD-FHA's division of Housing Production and Mortgage Credit, *FHA Homes 1970*, (Washington, D.C.: HUD, SOR-2, 1972). Most of the BLS data were found in U.S. Bureau of Labor Statistics, *Handbook of Labor Statistics, 1974* (Washington, D.C.: U.S. Government Printing Office, 1974). BLS provided unpublished data on the purchase price of homes. The various capital and operating components of the BLS composite index were combined using 1970 weights, published in U.S. Bureau of Labor Statistics, *Importance of Components in the Consumer Price Index, 1970-71* (Washington, D.C.: U.S. Government Printing Office, 1972).

Figure C-2

COMPARISON OF BLS AND FHA (NEW HOMES)
CAPITAL AND OPERATING COST INDEXES

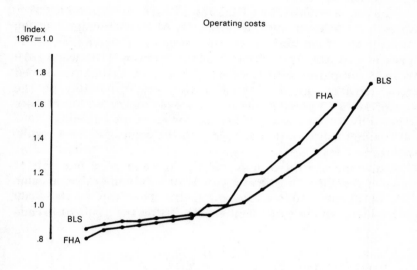

Operating costs

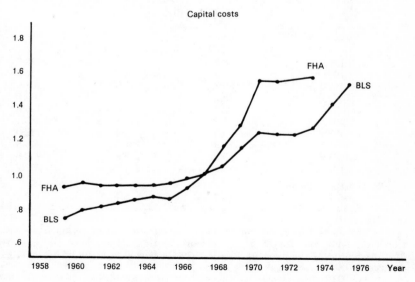

Capital costs

the independent variables. For predictive purposes, the auto-correlation evident in all the models is not a problem.[14] Also note that while the estimates using the BLS and FHA measures as dependent variables have statistically significant differences, the series themselves for P_0 and P_c over the observation period are highly correlated ($r > .9$ in each case).

The projections of the CPI, P_c and P_0 are given in table C-7.[15] Interestingly, even though the elasticity of P_c with respect to the CPI is greater than that for P_0, the change in P_0 over the decade is greater than that in P_c because of the jump in P_0 between 1970 and 1973 compared with that in P_c. The 1979 estimates seemed to give too large an increase over the decade, possibly on the order of 10 to 15 percent, because the extremely sharp increases of the early 1970s are embodied in the estimated models. As a final step in the estimation of P_c and P_0 the values are, as a result, revised downward.

Using the projected data and the average price per unit of service of dwellings in the stock in 1970 as a numeraire, a value of P_n of about 2.10 was determined.[16] This represents a 69 percent increase over the comparable P_n for the 1960-70 decade

Table C-7
PROJECTIONS TO 1979 OF THE CPI, P_c, AND P_0
(1967=100)

Year	CPI	P_c	P_0
1970	116.3	154.1	128.6
1971	121.3	152.0	136.8
1972	125.3	157.5	161.0
1973	133.3	155.7	161.0
1974	147.7	178.2	190.6
1975	161.2	204.8	215.1
1976	170.5	220.4	232.0
1977	179.8	237.8	248.8
1978	189.2	255.0	265.8
1979	198.2	271.8	282.2
Percentage change 1970-79	70.4	76.4	119.4

[14] The models were estimated using a first-order autocorrelation correction technique, and for P_c the parameter estimates changed significantly. The prediction of the average P_c for 1970-79, however, changed by less than 5 percent.

[15] The CPI projections are those from Data Resources, Inc., May 1976.

[16] See deLeeuw and Struyk, *The Web of Urban Housing*, chapter 4, for a full description of these computations.

($P_n = 1.24$). The prices just calculated then had to be converted to a 1960 base, since the distribution of the services defined for 1960 (which when updated through the 1966-70 simulations yields the base dwelling distribution of the 1970-80 simulations) is dependent on the 1960 average price level. Hence, P_c and P_o were multiplied by the radio of P_n in 1970 to P_n in 1960. Finally, the two prices were adjusted downward by 15 percent in keeping with the judgment that there was upward bias in the basic predictive models. The variable values resulting from this process are $P_c = 1.29$ and $P_o = 1.50$.

APPENDIX D
FULL RESULTS
OF SECTION 8
SIMULATION

Table D-1

GUIDE TO SECTION 8 SIMULATIONS

	High-minority								Low-minority							
	Rapid-growth				Slow-growth				Rapid-growth				Slow-growth			
	Elastic		Inelastic		Elastic		Inelastic		Elastic		Inelastic		Elastic		Inelastic	
Case Number[a]	Proportion New	Exist.	Proportion New	Exist.	Proportion New	Exist.	Proportion New	Exist.	Proportion New	Exist.	Proportion New	Exist.	Proportion New	Exist.	Proportion New	Exist.
I. Basic simulations[b]																
A. Proportional allocation scheme																
C1, C2	50	50														
C3, C4			50	50												
C5					50	50										
C6							50	50								
C7, C8									50	50						
C9, C10											50	50				
C11													50	50		
C12															50	50
B. Fair-share allocation scheme																
C13	50	50														
C14			50	50												
C15					50	50										
C16							50	50								
II. Policy variations																
A. Proportional allocation scheme																
All new[c] D1	100	0														
All new D2			100	0												

	Case[a]	New (%)	Existing (%)
All new	D3	100	0
All new	D4	100	0
No FMR ceiling[d]	D5	50	50
No FMR ceiling	D6	50	50
No FMR ceiling	D7	50	50
No FMR ceiling	D8	50	50
B. Fair-share allocation scheme			
1970–80[e]	D9	60	40
1970–80	D10	60	40
All new	D11	100	0
All new	D12	100	0
No FMR ceiling	D13	50	50
No FMR ceiling	D14	50	50
No FMR ceiling	D15	50	50
No FMR ceiling[f]	D16	50	50
No FMR ceiling[f]	D17	50	50

[a] The case numbers correspond to those used in the full tables of simulation results presented in appendixes C and D.
[b] All the basic policy simulations (C1–C16) are of a Section 8 program having 50 percent new units and 50 percent already existing units (50/50).
[c] Program consists of all newly-built units.
[d] This is a 50/50 program simulated without the maximum rent ceiling, although a maximum subsidy based on FMR is still in effect.
[e] These are simulations projecting Section 8 program from 1970 to 1980.
[f] FMR ceiling and maximum government subsidy restrictions are both removed.

Table D-2
FULL RESULTS, BASIC SECTION 8 POLICY SIMULATIONS

	Proportional Allocation										Fair-Share Allocation					
	High-Minority Rapid-Growth				High-Minority Slow-Growth		Low-Minority Slow-Growth				Low-Minority Rapid-Growth		High-Minority Rapid-Growth		High-Minority Slow-Growth	
	Elastic		Inelastic		Elastic	In-elastic	Elastic		Inelastic		Elastic	In-elastic	Elastic	In-elastic	Elastic	In-elastic
Case Number	C1	C2	C3	C4	C5	C6	C7	C8	C9	C10	C11	C12	C13	C14	C15	C16
Program Type	C^a	A^b	C	A	A	A	C	A	C	A	A	A	A	A	A	A
1. Participation rate	.50	1.00	.50	1.00	1.00	.50	.50	1.00	.50	1.00	1.00	.80	1.00	.75	1.00	.83
2. Average subsidy	28.89	23.85	26.92	15.35	33.90	33.13	36.92	27.95	28.90	24.18	27.22	21.28	42.70	38.47	37.99	33.86
3. Earmarking ratio—New	—	1.58	—	1.88	1.25	1.40	—	1.84	—	1.39	1.16	1.81	1.05	1.54	1.06	1.27
—Existing	.448	.474	.638	.268	.361	—	.479	.460	.379	.376	.437	.611	.641	.676	.645	.817
4. Average percentage change, quantity of services																
a. Participants—New	—	26.90	—	26.78	37.83	34.32	—	29.00	—	25.52	28.36	20.83	20.27	21.73	32.61	31.10
—Existing	12.65	20.23	8.01	7.99	20.38	—	21.14	25.09	20.56	28.30	29.73	33.44	71.04	66.76	41.57	24.82
b. All households	.75	2.38	.28	4.73	3.22	3.22	.26	3.83	.30	2.57	3.24	1.97	7.55	3.88	6.37	3.68
5. Percentage change, expenditures																
a. Participants—New	—	27.06	—	34.17	47.72	56.63	—	42.05	—	28.83	21.08	22.31	21.65	35.37	41.15	66.76
—Existing	17.36	19.30	25.12	5.23	19.28	—	26.11	24.15	48.74	47.26	22.25	31.31	68.24	74.61	51.26	63.75
b. All households	−.19	1.96	1.00	−.68	2.68	.84	.48	4.34	.94	2.43	4.47	.18	7.56	7.68	9.07	8.92
6. Percentage of increase in expenditures attributed to price inflation																
a. Participants	25.11	.53	66.52	14.45	8.94	29.06	20.72	15.45	62.67	25.70	0	5.77	.41	21.07	17.43	43.67

7. Average price per unit of service																
a. Participants																
1. Base	1.193	1.215	1.040	1.103	1.143	1.064	1.152	1.139	.837	1.127	1.231	1.122	1.218	1.083	1.092	.878
2. Policy—New	NP	1.24	NP	1.24	1.24	1.24	NP	1.24	NP	1.24	1.24	1.24	1.24	1.24	1.24	1.24
—Existing	1.245	1.187	1.24	1.006	1.115	NP	1.214	1.157	1.092	1.013	1.147	1.039	1.195	1.069	1.126	.970
b. All households																
1. Base	1.230	1.230	1.186	1.186	1.190	1.129	1.216	1.216	1.160	1.160	1.245	1.049	1.230	1.186	1.190	1.129
2. Policy	1.239	1.211	1.208	1.144	1.181	1.100	1.227	1.218	1.178	1.160	1.213	1.024	1.231	1.169	1.214	1.162
8. Number of units withdrawn																
a. Base	0	0	3	3	3	6	3	3	6	6	0	3	0	3	3	6
b. Policy	0	2	3	5	5	7	3	5	6	8	3	5	4	6	6	8
9. Number of new units																
a. Base	9	9	12	12	5	8	7	7	10	10	12	15	9	12	5	8
b. Policy	9	11	12	14	7	9	7	9	10	12	15	17	13	15	8	10
10. Number of blacks in zone 1																
a. Base	5	5	6	6	4	4	1	1	2	2	2	1	5	6	4	4
b. Policy	3	5	6	5	3	4	1	0	2	2	2	1	3	3	4	4

[a] Households have free choice regarding participation and new or existing housing.

[b] Some households are assigned to new units built under the program.

[c] Earmarking ratio is the ratio of the change in housing expenditure to subsidy received.

Table D-3
FULL RESULTS, SECTION 8 POLICY VARIATIONS[a]

	Proportional								Fair Share								
Program Type	100% New				No FMR Ceiling				1980		100% New		No FMR				
Growth Rate	Rapid Growth				Rapid Growth		Slow Growth		Rapid[c]	Slow	Rapid Growth		Rapid	Slow Growth		Rapid [b]	Slow [b]
Minority Proportion	High-Minority		Low-Minority		High-Minority		Low-Minority							High Minority			
Elasticity	E	I	E	I	E	I	E	I	I	I	E	I	E	E	I	E	E
Case Number	D1	D2	D3	D4	D5	D6	D7	D8	D9	D10	D11	D12	D13	D14	D15	D16	D17
1. Participation rate	1.00	1.00	1.00	1.00	.50	.50	.50	.50	1.00	1.00	1.00	1.00	.75	.833	.833	.875	1.00
2. Average subsidy	19.29	19.29	22.10	22.10	31.39	27.54	35.84	26.89	50.83	76.13	30.40	30.40	41.44	43.39	31.65	45.59	47.87
3. Earmarking ratio—New	1.053	1.545	.697	1.063	.493	.718	.585	.973	.778	1.10	.789	1.10	—	—	—	—	—
—Existing	—	—	—	—	—	—	—	—	.238	.773	—	—	.660	.742	1.028	.725	.819
4. Average percentage change, quantity of services																	
a. Participants—New	20.27	21.75	17.06	19.78	15.34	8.94	22.24	20.66	4.26	15.55	28.81	27.13	31.65	36.46	22.36	44.11	43.83
—Existing	—	—	—	—	—	—	—	—	17.46	43.22	—	—	—	—	—	—	—
b. All households	2.45	2.266	2.17	3.21	.09	.42	.51	.25	1.19	2.18	2.77	5.57	2.21	2.04	1.03	2.01	2.97
5. Average percentage change, expenditures																	
a. Participants—New	22.06	35.38	16.26	26.14	20.76	28.21	30.00	44.89	20.11	17.21	30.95	49.30	43.17	55.30	71.47	48.94	59.99
—Existing	—	—	—	—	—	—	—	—	8.10	51.55	—	—	—	—	—	—	—
b. All households	.63	1.486	1.732	2.12	.16	1.41	.89	.79	3.82	5.36	3.01	4.30	2.79	3.44	3.49	2.18	4.56
6. Percentage of increase in expenditures attributed to price inflation																	
a. Participants	5.18	31.68	0	20.13	23.79	65.15	24.59	60.42	41.62	7.29	5.30	35.34	21.12	30.27	56.95	6.76	14.96

	D1	D2	D3	D4	D5	D6	D7	D8	D9	D10	D11	D12	D13	D14	D15	D16	D17
7. Average price per unit of service																	
a. Participants																	
1. Base	1.226	1.115	1.245	1.178	1.193	1.040	1.152	.837	2.405	2.391	1.220	1.056	1.214	1.069	.794	1.215	1.092
2. Policy—New	1.24	1.24	1.24	1.24	—	—	—	—	2.780	2.780	1.24	1.24	—	—	—	—	—
—Existing	—	—	—	—	1.252	1.233	1.237	1.064	2.210	2.172	—	—	1.325	1.248	1.117	1.256	1.190
b. All households																	
1. Base	1.230	1.186	1.245	1.049	1.230	1.186	1.216	1.160	2.657	2.502	1.230	1.186	1.230	1.190	1.129	1.230	1.190
2. Policy	1.236	1.199	1.231	1.217	1.236	1.212	1.226	1.176	2.637	2.532	1.204	1.246	1.247	1.230	1.190	1.2	1.233
8. Number of units withdrawn																	
a. Base	0	3	0	3	0	3	3	6	1	0	0	3	0	3	6	0	3
b. Policy	4	7	5	8	0	3	3	6	6	5	8	11	3	4	6	4	5
9. Number of new units																	
a. Base	9	12	12	15	9	12	7	10	7	3	9	12	9	5	8	9	5
b. Policy	13	16	17	20	9	12	7	10	12	8	17	20	12	6	8	14	7
10. Number of blacks in zone 1																	
a. Base	5	6	2	1	5	6	1	2	4	2	5	6	5	4	4	5	4
b. Policy	5	5	1	1	3	3	0	2	4	1	5	4	3	3	4	3	3

[a]In cases D5-D8 and D13-D17, all households are free to choose between new and existing units. In the other cases, D1-D4 and D9-D12, some households are exogenously assigned to new units.

[b]No Fair Market Rent ceiling or maximum subsidy exists.

[c]There is a 60/40 mix of new and existing units under the program.

APPENDIX E
DEMAND FOR EXISTING SECTION 8 UNITS

In four cases in which all households are allowed free choice, acceptable solutions have not been reached. When none of the eligible households chooses new units, intense demand is concentrated on existing units qualifying for Section 8. Figure E-1 illustrates this point.

Existing dwellings qualifying for Section 8 subsidies must be to the right of (greater than) "ad" or 45 units of service, the minimum quality standard imposed by the program. The unit must also be below the hyperbola-shaped line "ab," which gives constant expenditure combinations of price multiplied by the quantity equal to the fair market rent (FMR). The demand for nonsubsidized units usually keeps the price of dwellings with output (Q) of 65 units or above (the minimum quality standard for new units) around P_n, the price per unit of service for a new unit. Thus, only units inside the area "abcd" meet both the Section 8 requirements. Consequently, a strong increase in demand may create more pressure than can be borne by the relevant range of existing units.

For example, if two or more households bid for the same dwelling, the landlord moves up the supply curve, "SS'" in the figure, until rent exceeds the FMR. The dwelling becomes ineligible for a subsidy and eligible households are no longer interested in it. The rent then drops below the FMR and the bidding among eligible households starts again. The process can be repeated until the time limit on searching for a solution is reached without every household being the unique occupant of one dwelling of its choice. This "boxing in" of the demand for eligible Section 8 units is one of the reasons for removing the FMR ceiling in one set of simulations. In the real world counterpart to this situation, the owner of the contested unit would probably choose between the competing households on a first-come, first-served basis.

Figure E-1

DEMAND FOR EXISTING SECTION 8 UNITS

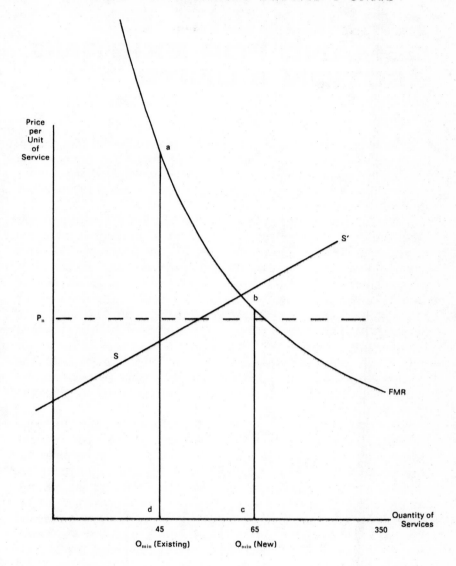

APPENDIX F
COMPARISON OF MARKET EFFECTS OF ALTERNATIVE HOUSING PROGRAMS IN TWO TYPES OF CITIES

Table F-1
ALTERNATIVE HOUSING PROGRAMS, TEXTILE CITY[a]

	Housing Allowance	Small Income Maintenance	Across-the-Board Construction Subsidy	One-step Construction Subsidy Housing Allowance	Rehabilitation Subsidy with Housing Allowance	Public Housing	Section 8 Proportional Assignment	Large Income Maintenance	Large One-step Construction Subsidy	Large Two-step Construction Subsidy
Impact on participants[b]										
Average monthly subsidy	$31	$31	c	$27	$22	$139	$24	$102	c	c
Participation rate	1.0	1.0		1.0	1.0	1.0	1.0	1.0		
Earmarking ratio[d]	.51	.33		.62	.61	e	1.03	.15		
Percentage change in housing expense	+24	+15		+26	+38	e	+23	+20		
Percentage change in housing quantity	+19	+10		+29	+30	+108	+24	+19		
Percentage change in housing price	+4	+5		−2	+7	e	+1	+2		
Price level before policy	1.210	1.210		1.207	1.207	.239	1.215	1.216		
Price after policy	1.259	1.269		1.181	1.287	e	1.214	1.236		
Number of model participants	10	10		7	7	2	4	11		
Impact on target population[f]										
Percentage change in housing expense	+24	+15	−3	+13	+24		+7	+27	−12	−19
Percentage change in										

housing quantity	+19	+10	+8	+17	+20	+16	+12	+21	+8	+3
Percentage change in housing price	+4	+5	-10	-4	+4	e	-5	+5	-18	-22
Price level before policy	1.209	1.209	1.209	1.209	1.209	1.209	1.209	1.209	1.209	1.209
Price after policy	1.259	1.269	1.086	1.162	1.254	e	1.152	1.269	.988	.948
Impact on all households										
Price level before policy	1.23	1.23	1.23	1.23	1.23	1.23	1.23	1.23	1.23	1.23
Price after policy	1.243	1.24	1.14	1.17	1.23		1.211	1.24	1.08	1.06
Change in number of model units withdrawn	+3	+1	+5	+3	0	+2	+2	+3	+5	+5
Change in number of new model units	+3	+1	+5	+3	0	+2	+2	+3	+5	+5
Change in number of black model households										
Zone 1	0	0	+1	0	+1	0	0	-1	0	-2
Zones 2-5	0	0	-1	0	-1	0	0	+1	0	+2
Costs as a percentage of housing allowance costs[h]	100	100	59	97	86	90	31	36	83	89

Note: For an explanation of footnote, see table 18.

Table F-2

ALTERNATIVE HOUSING PROGRAMS, GRAIN CITY[a]

	Housing Allowance	Small Income Maintenance	Across-the-Board Construction Subsidy	One-step Construction Subsidy Housing Allowance	Rehabilitation Subsidy with Housing Allowance	Public Housing	Section 8 Proportional Assignment	Large Income Maintenance	Large One-step Construction Subsidy	Large Two-step Construction Subsidy
Impact on participants[b]										
Average monthly subsidy	$26	$30	[c]	$22	$22	$143	$24	$103	[c]	[c]
Participation rate	.86	1.0		1.0	.75	1.0	1.0	1.0		
Earmarking ratio[d]	.98	.23		.23	.78	[c]	.88	.08		
Percentage change in housing expense	+46	+14		+35	+65	[c]	+38	+45		
Percentage change in housing quantity	+15	+4		+21	+38	+82	+27	+14		
Percentage change in housing price	+31	+10		+19	+20	[c]	+10	+28		
Price level before policy	.903	.858		.771	.766	.603	1.122	.872		
Price after policy	1.186	.941		.919	.920	[c]	1.140	1.113		
Number of model participants	6	7		5	3	2	4	7		

Impact on target population[f]										
Percentage change in housing expense	+44	+14	−17	+23	+19	°	+22	+48	−25	−14
Percentage change in housing quantity	+12	+4	−2	+10	+18	−18	+16	+14	−29	+5
Percentage change in housing price	+28	+10	−15	+11	+1	°	+5	+29	−23	−18
Price level before policy	.858	.858	.858	.858	.858	.858	.858	.858	.858	.858
Price after policy	1.101	.941	.731	.955	.863	°	.900	1.109	.660	.703
Impact on all households										
Price level before policy	1.160	1.16	1.16	1.16	1.16	1.16	1.16	1.16	1.16	1.16
Price after policy	1.212	1.18	1.06	1.13	1.13	1.160	1.16	1.21	1.02	1.03
Change in number of new model units	0	0	+1	+1	−2	+2	+2	0	+2	+3
Change in number of black model households										
Zone 1	0	0	+1	0	0	+1	0	−1	−1	0
Zones 2-5	0	0	−1	0	0	−1	0	+1	+1	0
Costs as a percentage of housing allowance costs[h]	100	135	127	146	114	183	62	463	148	174

Note: For an explanation of footnote, see table 18.

INDEX

Proportional assignment compared
to alternative programs, 63–64,
134–39, 144–47
Subsidies (direct cash payments to
landlords), iii, 5, 32, 34, 36–37,
50–51, 52, 58–59, 88
Slow-growth cities, underutilization
of existing stock, 54
Standard Metropolitan Statistical
Areas (SMSAs), 5–6, 20, 21, 23,
39, 112–13
Local cost of programs, 98
Spatial form, 6
Suburban zone, 25, 60, 66, 110
Supply-demand conditions
Demand figures for SMSA's, 6–9, 12
Demand pressure, 103
Demand stimulants, 44, 81, 140
Elastic-inelastic market com-
parisons, 26–28, 49–55, 57, 61,
78–81, 99–105, 134–39
Imbalances, 7, 10–14, 22, 28, 30, 60,
74, 80, 140–41
Landlord supply parameters, 19–20
1960 market, 77
Submarkets, 13–14
Supply schedule, 109
Supply stimulation (*see also* New
units), 11, 44, 67, 96, 109

Target population, 99, 100, 101, 102,
104
Defined, 101*n*
Travel times, 6, 18, 25, 108

Urban Institute's Housing Market
Simulation Model of 10-year
changes, 4–31
Advantages, 4–5
Description, 15–19
Prototype cities, 21–27

Welfare reform, iii, iv, 2, 60–70, 105
Carter Administration proposal, 63
"Demogrant" proposal (McGovern
campaign), 63
Family assistance plan (Nixon
Administration), 63
Small scale, 92
Withdrawals from stock, 109
Abandonment of still usable
structures, 3, 41, 53
Alternative programs and markets,
effect, 47, 51, 59, 62–69
passim, 79, 87, 99, 100, 101, 137,
139, 145
New unit construction, effect, 12,
29, 30, 43–44, 53, 69, 81, 83
1980 projection, 74, 88

Zones of metropolitan areas (*see also*
Suburban zone), 6, 25, 29
Inner city (zone 1), 24–25, 30, 66
Minority and poor household
locations, 13, 22, 24–25, 29,
37, 108
Zoning ordinances, 110